Cameos of the Western Front

Salient Points Five

Ypres Sector 1914–1918

By the same group of authors in The Cameos of the Western Front series*:

The Anatomy of a Raid
Australians at Celtic Wood, October 9th, 1917

Salient Points One
Ypres Sector 1914 - 1918

Salient Points Two
Ypres Sector 1914 - 1918

Salient Points Three
Ypres Sector 1914 - 1918

Salient Points Four
Ypres Sector 1914 - 1918

A Walk Round Plugstreet (revised edition)
Ypres Sector 1914 - 1918

Poets & Pals of Picardy
A Weekend on the Somme with Mary Ellen Freeman

A Haven in Hell
Everyman's Club, Poperinghe

In the Shadow of Hell
Behind the lines at Poperinghe

First published in Great Britain in 2009 by Pen & Sword Military
an imprint of Pen & Sword Books Ltd
47 Church Street, Barnsley
South Yorkshire S70 2AS

Copyright © Tony Spagnoly and Ted Smith, 2009
ISBN 978-1-84884-179-6

Printed and bound in England by CPI UK

Pen & Sword Books Ltd incorporates the Imprints of Pen & Sword Aviation, Pen & Sword Maritime, Pen & Sword Military, Wharncliffe Local History, Pen & Sword Select, Pen & Sword Military Classics and Leo Cooper.

For a complete list of Pen & Sword titles please contact
PEN & SWORD BOOKS LIMITED
47 Church Street, Barnsley, South Yorkshire, S70 2AS, England
E-mail: enquiries@pen-and-sword.co.uk
Website: www.pen-and-sword.co.uk

Cameos of the Western Front
Salient Points Five
Ypres Sector 1914 - 1918

by Tony Spagnoly and Ted Smith

With an introduction by
Guillaume Vandersande

Pen & Sword
MILITARY

CONTENTS

ACKNOWLEDGEMENTS

Firstly, a special Thank You to Nick Fear for his excellent photograph of the late Tony Spagnoly shown wearing his uncle's crucifix. Tony sadly but peacefully passed away before the completion of this book.

Gratitude is offered to Gary Fancy for his article on 2nd-Lieutenants Paul J Rodocanachi and Norman L Watt of the Royal Flying Corps from which much of the detail of their service records was taken.

Likewise to Peter Threllfall who was a source of inspiration as well as information on the Cheshires in the Wood cameo. Without the regular flow of his unbelievable amount of detail on the Regiment's 10th, 11th and 13th Battalions the cameo would never have seen the light of day.

Denis Otter, East Lancashire researcher, and Andy Mackay, both regular providers of all sorts of information, photographs and other materials to me and many others deserve more than due credit – the Lancashire Regiments could not find better representatives than they.

Patrik Indevuyst of the Shell Hole bookshop in Ypres deserves a special vote of thanks for an unlimited source of coffee as well as help, advice and information on all things relative to the effects of the Great War in Ypres and its surrounding villages [as well as his loan of a camera when the writer forgot to charge his camera's battery before leaving England]. Patrik was the cause of the contact being made with Philip Woets whose historical knowledge of what was Palingbeek Château, better known to Great War enthusiasts as White Château, is beyond belief and certainly merits thanks.

Patrick Roelens, Emmanuel Bril and Frederic Seynave are thanked for their willing co-operation in offering information, detail and help on their discoveries of the remains of Privates Harry Wilkinson and Richard Lancaster of the 2nd Battalion Royal Lancashire Fusiliers.

Gratitude is extended to Claude and Nelly Verhaeghe, proprietors of L'Auberge, the restaurant opposite the Ploegsteert Memorial, for their hospitality, help and the use of their premises as a base when in the area.

As always, many thanks for the excellent services offered by the staffs of the Imperial War Museum, the Commonwealth War Graves Commission and the National Archives.

Taken for granted, rarely mentioned, but not to be forgotten, are those who are responsible for the Internet together with the constructors and operators of Eurotunnel. What would life be like without them?

Most of all, our acknowledgements and thanks go to the men and women, both those who fell and those who survived, that endured the hardship and suffering of the Great War.

Ted Smith and, in his absence, Tony Spagnoly. March 2009.

INTRODUCTION

Being asked to write this introduction came as something of a surprise to me as my interest is primarily within the archives and activities of the Belgian Army in the Great War – as a researcher, but not as a writer.

My only knowledge of the British Army's involvement in the war is concerning its operations in Antwerp, Zeebrugge, Ostende and Nieuport in 1914 and 1918. Reading this book about individuals, raiding parties, burials, small actions, and day-to-day regimental life – all with maps to follow for those who visit the areas – is very different to studying maps and documents on strategies and tactics to determine whether important operations were intelligently conceived and implemented.

The stories contained in this book have brought my attention to the fact that many of the men who fought in the war, the Territorials, were really only civilians acting in the role of part-time soldiers, wearing the same uniforms as the regular soldier who themselves were just ordinary people in uniform with desires and aspirations the same as those of the civilian.

A military uniform gives to the person wearing it an image of professionalism and efficiency, a well-trained, disciplined aggressor, a fighting-man totally adept in the art of armed combat whether it be on land, at sea or in the air – someone prepared and ready to practice his skills in whatever conditions he finds himself in at any given time.

He is not thought of as having a mother, father, wife, son, daughter, niece, nephew or grandchildren. He's not a shopkeeper, cook, doctor, driver, mechanic, musician, labourer, accountant or candle-stick maker. He is a soldier, sailor or airman, a man in a uniform who fights to make his living – not much use to us to have around in peacetime, but very important to us in times of conflict.

But then, without his uniform, he is seen as just an ordinary person, and we are rarely prompted into thinking about what he does for a living,

How many of those 'ordinary persons' acting as part-time or regular soldiers knew in what country they were fighting during the war? How many had heard of Ypres, the Somme or the Western Front? They surely didn't know they were fighting in a battle for Messines or Passchendaele, and who amongst them ever knew they were taking part in the 'Race to the Sea', or had ever heard of the First, Second and Third Battles of Ypres?

I doubt if most of them even knew in what direction they were facing in a devastated agricultural area of mud, shellholes and trenches, surrounded by farmsteads and villages that were no more than piles of rubble entitled with English names to give those 'ordinary persons' some idea of what they were attacking or defending? And all this without the ability to move in daylight, being under constant threat of artillery bombardment or gas attack, living in dugouts in front line trenches and so-called billets in the back areas were the local communities did not speak a language they could understand and did not want them to be there anyhow.

They managed to deal with it for a long time and, when the war was over, they went back to where they came from to return to being 'ordinary persons' or to continue wearing a uniform as long as the Military would have them.

They left behind them devastated countries, and did their best to forget the war and the hardships they had experienced – but they did not forget their dead. Regimental Burial Plots became rudimentary cemeteries, individual and small groups of graves in the areas surrounding these cemeteries were collected and transferred to them. These were then individually designed and laid-out to become the Commonwealth War Grave Commission Military Cemeteries as we know them today.

I am sure that most Belgians are aware of these, as well as the many military extensions in their local communal cemeteries, fully recognising their importance to the British. They are to be found all over Belgian Flanders and Northern France, but their many mentions in this book and the burials in them during recent years of soldiers whose remains have been discovered are new to me. The fact that these soldiers' remains were buried with full military honours has emphasised the important place that the Great War holds in the hearts and minds of, not only the British, but to all the people of those countries who took part in that conflict.

Few of those who fought in that war remain with us today, but they and those who have long gone will not be forgotten. The Great War is no longer something of Living Memory but the coach- and car-loads of people, adult and infant alike, who flock to the battlefields of Belgium and France every year will always visit those cemeteries, ensuring that the memory is kept alive.

Books of the nature of this one will also help those visitors realise that soldiers, sailors and airmen were, and are, only 'ordinary persons' wearing uniforms and will help that remembrance too.

Guillaume Vandersande. November 2008

DEDICATION

This book is dedicated to the memory Tony Spagnoly,
Author, Researcher, Battlefield Guide and
all things related to the Great War of 1914-1918.
He passed away quietly and peacefully
on 5 October 2008

EDITORS NOTE

A few years back Tony Spagnoly suggested that, given time, we should each write a book on our individual reflections on Ypres and the Great War. Both books were to be based on a weekend trip to Ypres calling on what we had produced in the Salient Points series of books, what we would liked to have featured in them, subjects tabled for further publications and whatever else we felt merited inclusion. We agreed that we would read each other's versions so as not to produce similar editions.

Tony was a poet with a remarkable imagination and the natural ability to write from his heart. His wealth of knowledge on the Great War, his deep feeling for the men who served, the civilians who suffered, the towns and villages that were razed, and the very ground upon which all this happened, was let loose like an opening flood gate. He produced 14 chapters in no time at all while I was still struggling through my fourth.

His 'draft' is a masterpiece, showing just how deeply he felt for, and thought of, not only of those who fought and died in the Ypres Salient, but the devastating effects it had on the lives of those who were involved through no desire or fault of their own.

The following pages give a foretaste of his manuscript, featuring just the book's Title, Preface and Chapter 1. The page-count of his work, bearing in mind it was only a draft, is not sufficient enough to produce a book, and his unique style of writing eliminates the possibility of anyone taking on the task of finalising it – but it would (and will) make a superb booklet.

Ted Smith. October 2008

A PERSONAL ODYSSEY
by Tony Spagnoly

PREFACE

This book about Ypres and those very deep thoughts it inspires in many of us, was conceived as far back as September 1977 when the old town of Ypres was crowded to celebrate the 50th Anniversary of the inauguration of the Menin Gate in 1927, and the 60th Anniversary of the Third Battle of Ypres – the bid to capture Passchendaele, a word which has now found its place, a very sombre one, in the English language.

I had been in the company of the late Rose Coombs, and the late John Giles at the Cloth Hall when John suddenly felt ill and I assisted him back to his hotel which was near the railway station square. I felt very concerned but, on his insistence, I did not call a doctor as all he wanted was to lie down and rest. John had been ill for some years following his first heart attack in this historic old town. "Couldn't think of a better place to die" he would often joke.

As for me, after seeing him to his bed, I worried about him all night. However, John bounced back in that special way he had and, at breakfast, was his usual jovial and ebullient self. I was very relieved.

He had said the night before, whilst I was attempting to emulate Florence Nightingale, that completing his book The Ypres Salient. Then and Now. In 1974 had given him the renewed energy and vigour to complete the other books in the series he had planned which had given him much pleasure and a real point to his life, a truly important point. John, although always suffering, had the grit and determination to stay with us a further 14 years until he passed on quietly in 1991. He was sadly missed.

It made me think, even then, we have to have aiming points in our lives, or we leave nothing behind.

Rose Coombs will always be remembered for her Before Endeavour Fades, a splendid work which has introduced thousands to the joys and mysteries of the old battlefields in Flanders, Picardy and elsewhere.

I don't expect this book of indulgent thought to stand comparison with these two giants who have left us, but in its humble way, will continue their work, and help some others along the way of understanding and remembrance.

That's all one can wish for.

Tony Spagnoly. May 2004

A PERSONAL ODYSSEY

Chapter 1
The Road to Ypres

A NOTHER REFLECTIVE BOOK about Ypres which may incur the charge of wearing that time honoured Ypres badge of grief on one's sleeve. Ypres, that special town so hallowed to the British race which gladdens and saddens me each time I visit, so much so that I have long since passed the point of trying to analyse with any degree of rationale the emotions that it generates.

Ypres was a place of a thousand lost hopes and shattered illusions for a past generation of young men from all over the world. From our vantage point in time we can only view the horrific slaughter of the world's finest in this tiny corner of Belgian Flanders in a kind of dazed wonderment. Giving this area the healing balm of the serene title 'The Immortal Salient' is not enough to assuage the pain. Just repeating these simple words can in no way sanitize the world-shattering events that took place here, the brutality or the suffering. This laurel leaf of sorrow does not change that, how could it? Ypres was, and will forever be, that 'vale of tears' of British arms which laid claim to the cherished hopes of 150,000 young lives in the muddy obscenity which was this battlefield where the landscape and features just sank into a morass of mud.

Since 1914 it would seem that society has been on a slippery slope of increasing decline having never recovered from the seismic happening that was the Great War. Those dramatic years of 1914-18 are beyond the recall of most people living to-day, yet its scar has left an indelible mark upon society in a most profound way even though the guns have been silent now for over 90 years.

That narrow strip which constituted the trenches, snaked its relentless way from the North Sea coast to the Swiss frontier over 400 miles distant. Young men from both sides burrowed deep within this tortured earth, glowering at each other across No-Man's Land, hoping to escape the shards of metal released by one side upon the other and probably at odds to understand how they came to be there. Nowhere was this more marked than around Ypres where the initial urgency of the German invader's attacks soon subsided to a collective theme of 'sitting it out' for the duration in face of the British obstinacy. They, in their turn, had suffered too much loss to their old professional army during 1914 and 1915 to be anything less than obdurate. The German foe was going nowhere, certainly not through Ypres anyway. The British Army that still remained, ably assisted by the splendid Canadians in 1915 and 1916, forged a magnificent resolve to keep this corner of their little ally inviolate from the invader's tread, no matter how heavy the cost. So a monumental price would be paid, Ypres would endure and the British Army would bar the way. Other sectors of the long front line would sway back and forth with the impetus of great battles but at Ypres, retreat was not an option, a mountain of dead and missing would not allow it. A mammoth exercise in mass obstinacy perhaps, but a magnificent one which we view from to-day's perspective with awe and wonderment.

These were my overwhelming thoughts as the car I had hired from Ostend after my evening sea-crossing hammered down the tarmac road between Dixmuide and Ypres. As evening turned to night we neared the old battle lines and I was reminded of the American writer Scott Fitzgerald's powerful comment in his classic book Tender is the Night when his hero remarks on the British and their agonies on the Western Front during his post-war visit to the battlefields: "It could never be done again" he says, "Not in a long time". I wonder about that sometimes. Men and nations do not change. Pride in one's country is a very potent force. One remembered a national press poll taken at the time of the Falklands fervour in 1982 when Britain's youth topped those throughout Europe willing to enlist at a time of national emergency.

Sometimes, tragic thoughts about the war can be interwoven with irrelevancies. Was it not from Ypres where the Flemish weavers were exiled to East Anglia at the time of the mediaeval religious wars several hundred years back, in order to set up a prosperous weaving industry in that part of England? They took many of their customs and language with them. Two word's that always springs to mind and are a firmly established are 'Tissue d'Ypres', which referred to a special type of fabric. This, in the fullness of time, 'americanised' into 'diaper'. I can never hear this word used without recourse to the Cloth Hall and the Menin Gate. Valid thinking I suggest. Those worthy Burghers of the Middle Ages have given way to their wealthy counterparts to-day. The old town is thriving and affluent and strives manfully to make its mark in the modern world with a seemingly ever more youthful population having taken over from the more stolid agricultural-based work force stretching from the immediate post-war period to-day.

Always a pleasure to visit in its own right, Ypres is caught in a web of its own, not afraid to face up to its bloody past of recent memory and to mark its place in the sun of a peaceful modern Belgium. It has fought hard to retain its unique individuality, remote from the war-torn past. It is a beautiful town as befits a former jewel of the Middle Ages. At certain times of the year the international motor rally that centres on Ypres is not to everyone's taste. The roar of the combustion engine and smell of diesel in the air does not equate with the peace and tranquility of the little cemeteries outside the ramparts walls and one might be forgiven for thinking perhaps Ypres is not quite the place for the pilgrim to be, but the event is undoubtedly good for the town and its business. With the influx of visitors it generates and, as the war hereabouts was fought to ensure such freedoms, who could object? Certainly not I.

Nor does the massive and ever-increasing financially successful Bellewaarde Theme Park at Hooge fit into this schematic. As one who was with the late Baron de Vynke of Hooge 20-years ago when he first announced a small initial parcel of his land had been set aside for such a purchase, and that the memorial to the King's Royal Rifle Corps would have to be moved slightly along the Menin Road to accommodate, a slight chill descended upon the spirit, because any discerning soul would know this could be the proverbial 'thin end of the wedge' and that things were about to change in these modem times. This bloodied and hallowed sector of Hooge and Château Wood would be launched from its Great War perspective into the 20th Century, However, all forebodings of 1977 apart, who cannot admit that after many years of successful operating and, seeing the complete happiness instilled in thousands of happy and blissful children many in coach loads from as far south as Paris and other points of Europe, the venture has been a resounding success? The many hundreds of young soldiers from both sides who lie at their rest here can rest easy. Their sacrifice has not been diluted by all of this in any form, perhaps, in a strange way, it has been honoured further - what could be more fitting than in perfect peace and tranquility happy children play upon the hidden graves of the fallen? Dramatic? I think not, because it is true.

When peace returned to this shattered land it must have been difficult for the local government to know what to do with the ruined waste they had inherited. To hide and shroud the angry scars in their midst a decision was made to rebuild in a precise and devoted manner a modern Ypres in the Dutch/Flemish gabled style of old from the original plans and drawings kept in safety throughout the war years in Northern France.

The British, in parallel with the prodigious efforts of their allies, created a splendid 'schematic' of their own with several hundred garden-style cemeteries, massive memorials to the missing and parks of remembrance. They could never bring back the generation they aimed to commemorate, but what they could do would visibly aid the message of remembrance, bringing into sharp focus one of the great adages of Mother Church: "In Remembrance Lies Life Eternal" which was certainly a message of hope for all who grieved and the mass of pilgrims in the after-years who would visit.

When involved in a mass expression of loss and sacrifice, especially at such a unique daily sounding of Last Post at the Menin Gate, it is difficult not to detect an immense inner frustration of inadequacy at not being able to grieve deeply enough. He felt it often and was sure he was not alone in this respect. It seems we are unable to conjure up the right thoughts or combination of words in order to do real justice to this total expression of sacrifice, duty, loyalty and patriotism we view. Patriotism: a word not easily utterable in to-day's Britain. English may be the mother language of Shakespeare, Chaucer and Milton, but no permutation of words it seems are readily available to sum-up our feelings. I suspect many of the young men remembered at Ypres would feel exactly the same. They too might be lost for an apt phrase. They died in many ways, for many ideals and in many and varied places. In their agonies as that final mist descended to ease their tortured beings, many things would have been on their minds but sacrifice and the glory of the flag might not have been paramount.

All these thoughts were in my head as the car drew nearer to the old town. Images a-plenty had flashed past keeping pace with the measured sound of the tyres along the ribbed tarmac road. How many from that past generation had made the same journey along this stretch of road which had separated British arms from those of our French and Belgian Allies? They, in their time, cold, tired, hungry, sore and sweating from the burden of a heavy load. Certainly not the comfortable surrounding I enjoyed.

In another time-zone, another place, perhaps even another life, that could have been him and his fellows. But then life is complex enough without adding to the conundrum. He only had the drooping lids heavy after a seven-hour journey from London to contend with, they had had the relentless Flemish rain, the dark lit by the odd Verey light or enemy shell which might blot out everything - such was the lottery of life then. Perhaps the jocular banter of a more uplifted comrade to maintain morale and lift the spirits. No. The road to Ypres in the war years was hardly paved with gaiety, and his spirit was beginning to project this.

Ypres loomed large through the night sky ahead but even the evening mist could not shroud the illuminated Flemish Freedom Tower near Dixmuide as it stood proud and erect from the dank fields. Glancing quickly at it, he was reminded that it was constructed to honour the war dead of Flanders. But other agencies had different agendas and it soon became a symbol for a political expression, a small nation's quest for a national identity, a catalyst to air the grievance between different factions of the community. It has since become a focal point for the gathering of politically active right-wing parties from all over Europe. The young men of Belgium who fell and died in the area of the 'inundation' between the sea and Bixschoote, north-west of Ypres, need sleep no less easy because of it. Sacrifice comes at a price. Boesinghe Church and its tenuous story of Royalty flashed-by in the dusk, but I would return here at another time.

The famous bridge over the Ypres-Yser Canal, where began the 1917 advance to Passchendaele, the long low hump of the canal bank workings, the white blur of the first British cemeteries like so many transient ghosts in the dusk, slipped by giving me cause to wonder at those army cartographers and staff 'wallahs' in those early days allocating names for nondescript locations that would live forever in the history of the 1914-15 British Army Campaign in Flanders. Bard Cottage, Talana Farm [an echo of the Veldt] Essex Farm [now the most visited place after the Menin Gate for pilgrims and visitors to the Salient], Duhallow A.D.S. Cemetery - all were there and gone in a moment before the majestic mediaeval profile of the Cloth Hall, St. Martins and other ecclesiastical glories proudly basking in the lights of Ypres demanded attention. A final thought as I readied myself for the next stage of my journey - much had happened at Ypres and untold thousands of hopes blighted here, but the spirit of this lovely place had survived. The very essence of this jewel of the Middle Ages had surmounted tragedy to delight and move us all after so many years. How could we not but stay faithful to her and to 'them' in return? See what I mean about making our concerns on the sleeve so apparent.

Salvation Corner and all its associations, and the Dead End of the Canal at Tattenham Corner swept by as my anticipation increased when the car, as if in tune with my hopes, reached the almost deserted square on cue: I was here, and the bubbling spirit knew no bounds. The cab driver grinned as he was given a large tip and bade a cheery "Goodnight' by his passenger.

The remnants of Yprois Café Society remained to drag-out that last coffee of the night and watch through baleful eyes in a way unique to the Continental who views almost by instinct a foreigner trudging off like a lost soul to find his hotel for the night. The native also knows the missions most of the Britons are here for and respectfully acknowledges it. The square, usually the hub of Ypres life, is now empty and basks only in an eerie light so much in keeping with the ghost of another time who will 'people' the town during the night hours. He stood and stared at the now empty square from the steps of the hotel. The ghosts, if they were there, will be friendly. Will Bird, the Canadian military writer who served around Passchendaele in 1917, had recorded his experiences in a book entitled Ghosts Have Warm Hands after a return to Ypres in the post-war years, so he felt it too.

However, even the enchantment of Ypres can't hold back the onrush of sleep - nature's 'Velvet Glove', and there were more days ahead so he bade a good night to the silent square and those who 'roamed' it and turned aside.

Bed was calling.

. . . .

On 7 June 1999 a ceremony took place at the Ploegsteert Memorial inaugurating the sounding of Last Post at 7 pm on the first Friday of every month.

Organised and implemented by the local community through its Comité du Memorial de Ploegsteert, the monthly ceremony was devised to show their gratitude to, and to honour the memory of, the many thousands of Allied troops who made the ultimate sacrifice during the Great War of 1914–1918.

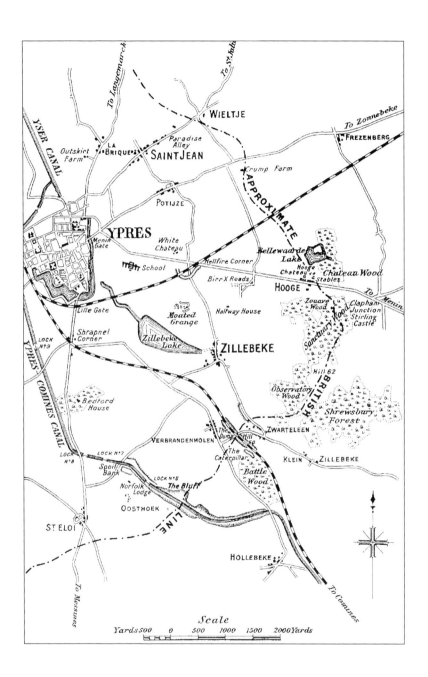

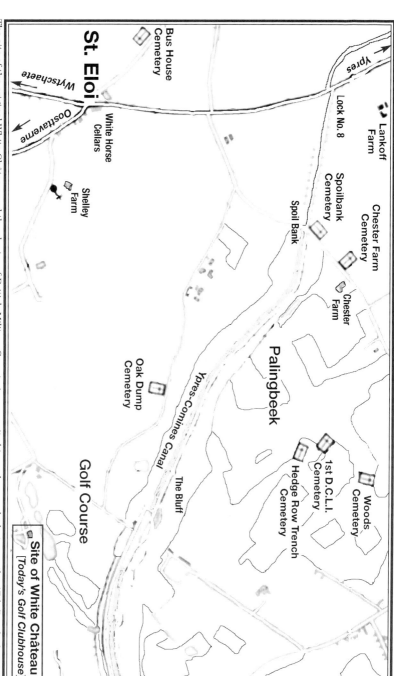

The site of the original White Château and the cluster of British Military Cemeteries now sited in and around what were the 47th (London) Division's boundaries at the opening of the Battle of Messines in June 1917.

Map labels:

St. Eloi
Wytschaete
Oosttaverne
White Horse Cellars
Bus House Cemetery
Shelley Farm
Lankoff Farm
Lock No. 8
Ypres
Chester Farm Cemetery
Spoilbank Cemetery
Spoil Bank
Chester Farm
Palingbeek
Oak Dump Cemetery
Ypres-Comines Canal
The Bluff
1st D.C.L.I. Cemetery
Hedge Row Trench Cemetery
Woods Cemetery
Golf Course

Site of White Château
[Today's Golf Clubhouse]

Young men of London should not be asked "go ye and do likewise,"
but "Go ye and train yourselves to do as well, but differently."
The Viscount ESHER, G.C.B., G.C.V.O., P.C.

1
A LONDON IRISH CRUCIFIX AND WHITE CHATEAU
Rifleman Vincent Sabini, 1/18th (County of London) Battalion
(London Irish Rifles), White Château, Hollebeke, 7 June 1917

THE 5TH INFANTRY BRIGADE, the London Regiment, 2nd London Division moved to France on 9-10 March 1915.[1] Its four battalions, the 17th (Poplar and Stepney), 18th (London Irish), 19th (St. Pancras) and 20th (Blackheath) disembarked at Le Havre and made their way to Cassel to await their sister battalions of the 4th and 6th Brigades who had been delayed in England. Before they left, the 4th and 6th's destination changed to Béthune, so the 5th left for Cassel on London omnibuses, with the four battalions needing a total of 168 buses in all to cope with its muster.

An extract from the Divisional History notes:

... the vast procession of 'buses loaded with men in the shaggy grey or pie bald goatskin coats, just served out to them, looked like a glorified 'Wild West Show' rather than like British Infantry going to the front and caused great amusement to the men and to their comrades of the other units of the Division.

In Béthune the Division, renamed the London Division, was attached to the British 2nd Division for trench acclimatisation (its name changed to avoid confusion with the latter), then entered the line on 20 April. On 11 May its name was changed again to The 47th (London) Division, its Brigades designated the 140th, 141st and 143rd respectively before, on 24 May it saw action in the Battle of Festubert,

Toward the end of August, the Division spent the better part of three weeks digging trenches, making ready for the Battle of Loos before taking intensive training for the battle where, on 25 September it launched its part in the attack.[2]

Ruins of Festubert village.

Loos in ruins.

After the battle it spent its winter in the Loos Salient, under the experience of frequent artillery duels, and mining activity, with the constant threat of gas attacks ever present.

Its memory of Christmas 1915 was one of:

Mines and counter-mines, hurricane bombardments, and mud – liquid, penetrating mud that flowed in over in over the top of knee-boots and sent many men down the line with trench feet ...

1916 proved to be an active year for the Division. On 4 January it relieved the French 18th Division at Loos, the town in ruins with only its cellars usable as billets. In mid-February, it moved to Corps Reserve, then to G.H.Q. before, in early March, taking over the Covinchy/Souchey sector where sniping and trench mortar duelling became a daily routine. On 26 April the Germans blew their first mine in the area, then mining and counter-mining became the norm, with the infantry repulsing attacks and launching counter-attacks whilst doubling-up as carrying parties for the tunnelling companies.

On 26 May the Division went into reserve, with casualties of 63 officers and 2,044 ranks killed, wounded or missing.

Back in the Angres sector in early June, it spent its time in diversionary operations to conceal the activity in preparation for the Battle of the Somme. Relieved by the Royal Naval Division on 18 July it went to rest billets, leaving the 141st Brigade as divisional reserve to the Navy. At the end of July, with the 141st back in its muster, It went into training in the St. Riquier area to join the now one-month-old battle. Once ready it moved to Baiseaux, joined III Corps and immediately went into another intensive three-week training period rehearsing for an attack on *High Wood*. Moving into the line on 10-11 September its London Irish (18th) and Poplar and Stepney (17th) Battalions attacked on the 15th and found themselves involved in a desperate fight for every foot of the advance on the wood. Casualties were high but, against all odds, *High Wood* was taken and cleared of the enemy by one o'clock in the afternoon.

21 September saw the brigades back in the Baiseaux area, the Division now reduced to 111 officers and 1,471 Other Ranks.

Refitted and with fresh drafts, it was back in the line on the 29th, its target – the capture of Eaucourt l'Abbaye which, unsuccessful in its first attempt on 1 October, it captured the following day.

After heavy losses in failed attacks on the Butte de Warlencourt the Division was relieved on 9 October having lost 296 officers and 7,745 other ranks killed, wounded or missing while involved in the Battle of the Somme.

On 10 October it moved northward into Belgium where, on the 19th, its 140th and 142nd Brigades took over *The Bluff* and *Hill 60* sectors from the Australian 2nd and 4th Divisions with the 141st held in Divisional Reserve.

The Bluff Craters.

Hill 60.

The Divisional front, one of just 2,300 yards, ran from the Ypres-Comines Canal on the right – inclusive of the *Bluff Craters* edging the canal – to north of the Ypres-Comines Railway on the left where, overlooked by the German occupied *Hill 60*, the troops suffered constant casualties from snipers. The weather proved to be as aggressive as the enemy when after a month of mine explosions, artillery shelling and extremely heavy frost, conditions became practically unbearable.

10 December saw the arrival of drafts from England amongst whom was 24-year old Rifleman Vincent Sabini, a devout London-born Catholic who had enlisted in the 18th (London Irish) Battalion in the January of 1916. For him and the rest of the Division the year closed quietly enough, but New Year's day 1917 brought with it heavy shelling along the whole front, seriously damaging trench systems.

Apart from this, Vincent Sabini's first experience of life at the front was being under daily artillery and trench mortar activity throughout the month which, combined with the rain and snow, made life intolerable, with the troops repairing trenches and working desperately hard in the frequent effort of evacuating their many casualties. Hard frost in early February made life even harder in the ice-bound trenches, and the back areas were suffering too, enemy shells registering narrow-gauge railways, causing transport problems for moving supplies and materials to the front. All this apart, a number of successful raids were implemented, one of which saw Rifleman Sabini take part in what was more like a pitched battle than

A stretch of the Ypres-Comines Canal in the 47th Division's sector.

a raid. The Germans were expecting some form of action and, with its artillery ready, and a battalion of storm troops brought in as close supports, they waited, fully prepared for it to begin. The London Irish were under gunfire as soon as they began their move up to the line and, on attacking, were met with a 'nut-cracker' barrage on both front and support lines. The enemy storm troops were brought up immediately and Sabini and his compatriots were involved in a close-quarter battle in the German reserve line with heavy casualties being taken on both sides. It ended with the London Irish taking 18 prisoners while destroying dugouts and emplacements, the downside being they suffered about 160 of all ranks killed, wounded or missing.

On 9 April a reorganisation of the Divisional Front began, taking the 47th Division astride the Ypres-Comines Canal. From then on the area was intermittently shelled, the strain on the troops increasing day by day, with no one able to count on uninterrupted rest. The troops began to sense that something important was due to happen in the near future. More frequent investigations of the enemys lines, increased activity in the air, regular visits to the forward areas by the Divisional Commander and his Staff, High Command Staff showing increased interest in the Division's positions as well the enemy's opposite them – all indicated some form of important offensive was in the offing. Then British artillery started regular destructive shoots on enemy lines and local road traffic increased with all sorts of units, *materiels* and supplies bringing a form organised chaos to the area.

By mid-May all concerned knew the details of the forthcoming Second Army Offensive and orders were issued accordingly – in brief, to capture and occupy the Messines Ridge, a formidable enemy occupied line of high ground stretching from Hill 60 southward to the fortified village of Messines.

Each Army Corps was made aware of its objectives and, likewise, each division its attack boundaries. The 47th were to attack astride the Ypres-Comines Canal with its 142th and 140nd Brigades manning the northern and southern sectors respectively. Two battalions of the 141st Brigade would be put under the command of the attack Brigades, the Poplar and Stepney (17th) with the 140th, and the Blackheath (20th) operating with the 142nd. The principal objectives for the brigades were, on the 142nd front, the two Spoil Banks and the canal bank and, on the 140th's, the *White Château* and stables and a section of the *Damme Strasse*. While these brigades underwent intensive attack rehearsals in the Steenvoorde area, the 141st manned the Divisional Front.

On 4 June the attack troops began their move into the line and, by 5 pm on the 6th, all units were in their alloted positions.

47th (London) Division

18th Battalion London Irish (Divisional Reserve)

Divisional Boundary

St Eloi

WhiteHorse Cellars

41st Division

Shelley Farm

Lankhof Farm

Lock No. 8

Lock No. 7

6th Battalion

Spoil Bank

Norfolk Lodge

20th Battalion

Chester Farm

La Chappelle

15th Battalion

Ypres – Comines Canal

British Front

German Front

8th Battalion

7th Battalion

23rd Battalion

21st Battalion

1st Objective

24th Battalion

Bluff Craters

22nd Battalion

Divisional Boundary

23rd Division

White Château

2nd Objective

1st Objective

2nd Objective

1st Objective

British Front

German Front

The 47th Division's Battalion positions within the Divisional Boundaries on 6 June 1917, awaiting the opening of the Battle of Messines due to launch at 3.10 am the following morning.

6

After six months in Belgium, Vincent Sabini, rooky Territorial or not, felt more like a London Irish 'Old Sweat' in the now battle-hardened, 18th Battalion.

The 6th June found him in Divisional Reserve manning a position west of the Ypres-Comines Canal running on a line south westward from Lock No. 8, in the direction of Vormezeele awaiting the opening of the battle due to launch at 3.10 am the following morning.

Of the 19 mines triggered at zero hour, the nearest to the 47th Divisional front were those at St. Eloi to its right and *Hill 60* and the *Caterpillar* to its left. The noise of the triggered mines, combined with the massive supporting artillery gunfire and the rattle of machine guns was deafening, with the eerie glare of the explosions and the flashes of the guns remaining an unforgettable memory to all who experienced it. Under this ceiling of unnatural light in the early morning, the infantry troops stormed across No-Man's Land to the enemy trenches, overcoming all opposition they met along the whole length of the Messines Ridge.

On the 47th Division's front the 7th and 8th battalions of 140th Brigade quickly met and overcame all obstacles until *White Château* was reached. The attack was held up here for a time but was successfully completed after the third attempt. Passing through for the Second Phase of the operation the supporting 15th and 16th Battalions met heavy opposition but succeeded in taking their objectives in the scheduled time, digging in and holding every foot of the ground they had taken.

The 24th and 25th Battalions of 142th Brigade also proceeded well, reaching and consolidating all their objectives. The 21st and 23rd in their advance through for the Second Phase met considerable opposition in attempting to cross the canal to link with the 140th Brigade south of it. Although reaching and holding their trench objectives, their left flank was exposed, the advance being held back by a combination of machine gun fire from concealed positions in the *Spoil Bank* together with problems encountered by the British 23rd Division in clearing the enemy from *Battle Wood* on the left of the 47th's Divisional Boundary. British artillery pounded this area throughout the whole of the afternoon and an attack was launched early that evening, but made little progress.

Later the 18th London Irish were called up from their reserve positions and cleared all this resistance before digging in and consolidating the line. During their attack a German bullet from the *White Château* area shattered Vincent Sabini's knee, and his involvement in the war was suddenly and painfully brought to an abrupt end.

P. T. & L., London, E.C.   Army Form B. 2067.
(A9520) Wt. W2500 PET/35600/13,8/ Sch. 41
Forms/E &/5

Serial No. *391*

CHARACTER CERTIFICATE OF No *593530*

Rank *Rfn.*   Name *Vincent Sabini.*

_____ Regiment,

Born in the Parish of *King's Cross*

near the Town of *London* in the

County of *London* on the

date *1890*

Trade as stated by him on enlistment *Carman.*

* DESCRIPTION ON LEAVING THE COLOURS

Height *5* ft. *6* in.   Identification Marks :—

Complexion *Dark*

Eyes *Brown*   *A/6 o88o23*

Hair *Black*   *Sep4*

Signature of Soldier

Vincent Sabini

* To prevent impersonation.

In the event of any doubt arising as to the *bona fides* of the bearer, the above description and signature should be carefully compared with present appearance and handwriting.

Vincent Sabini's Army Form B. 2067 (recto) giving basic character detail ...

8

Date of Enlistment ___ 12 . 1 . 16

Proceeded on Furlough pending transfer to the Army

Reserve, or Discharge on ___

Passed medically fit for the Army Reserve on ___

Due for Transfer to the Army Reserve on ___

Due for final Discharge on ___ JUN 1918

Cause of Transfer or Discharge ___

Campaigns, Medals and Decorations

HOME 12 . 1 . 16 to 12 . 1 . 16

24 . 8 . 16 to 9 . 12 . 16

10 . 12 . 16 to 11 . 10 . 17

12 . 10 . 17 to 11 . 6 . 18

Educational and other Certificates, and dates ___

14 Local Office

Policy issued

No. ___ C . 05 8 0 0 3 .

44/KP/86 9004

... and (verso)) his service and discharge record.

Army Form B. 2079.

WARNING.—*If you lose this Certificate a duplicate cannot be issued.*

N.B.—*Any person finding this Certificate is requested to forward it, in an unstamped envelope, to the Secretary, War Office, London. S.W.*

Certificate of discharge of No. *593530* (Rank) *Rfn*

(Name) *Vincent Sabini*

(Regiment) 18TH BATTN., LONDON REGT.

who was enlisted at *Paddington*

on the *12 . 1 .* 19 *16*

He is discharged in consequence of _____
no longer physically fit for War Service.

Para. 392 (XVII) King's Reg^ns 1912

after serving *1* years *293* days with the Colours, and
_____ years _____ days in the Army Reserve.

(Place) *London*   Signature of)
                          Commanding) *Wm Alley Major*
(Date) 1 JUN 1918   Officer)

*Description of the above-named man on 1 1 JUN 1918 when
he left the Colours.

Age *27 8/12*   Marks or Scars, whether on face
                       or other parts of body.
Height *5. 6'*
Complexion *Dark*
Eyes *Brown*
Hair *Black*

* Should agree with the description on Character Certificate, Army Form B. 2067
A.P. & S.D., Alex./No. 695/27: 4: 17/5000 (3931/47) W. M. & Co.

Vincent Sabini's Certificate of Discharge – irreplaceable if lost.

10

Passed back for treatment through the chain of Regimental Aid Posts, Dressing Stations, Casualty Clearing Stations and onto a Military Hospital in northern France he eventually ended up back in England on 12 October 1917 for treatment at the Manchester Hospital where the bullet was removed and the shattered knee was rebuilt. Nevertheless, he was only ever able to walk again with the aid of a walking stick.

London Irish Rifleman Vincent Sabini never returned to the front, spending seven months under treatment and convalescence before

being discharged on 11 June 1918 as being "No longer physically fit for war service". He kept the bullet that ended his time as a soldier and had it re-worked as a crucifix. He wore it for the rest of his life, believing the bullet that caused his injury was something that possibly saved his life in a battle which cost the 47th Division 2,303 casualties of all ranks killed, wounded or missing.

It certainly eliminated him from the division's actions on the Menin Road and Westhoek Ridge during the July Passchendaele offensive and from actions at Oppy, Gavrelle and Bourlon Wood later in the year. He was also spared the Division's retreat from Cambrai following the German offensive of March 1918.

Rifleman Vincent Sabini was to experience none of that. He had done his bit, paid his dues and suffered the consequences.

Rifleman Vincent Sabini in the grounds of Manchester Hospital whilst recovering from the wound to his shattered knee.

He rarely spoke of his wartime experiences but, when he did, he always mentioned the 'White House' as he called White Château, with its link to his wound and thereby his crucifix, a symbol of the event which he believed was instrumental in saving him from the fate which befell so many of his London Irish comrades. He wore the crucifix until he died peacefully at the age of 90 in 1981. His nephew, Tony Spagnoly, inherited the crucifix.

Photograph by Nick Fear.

Vincent Sabini's crucifix, made from the German bullet which caused his injury, worn by his nephew Tony Spagnoly.

Co-author of this book and others in *The Cameos of the Western Front* series, Tony Spagnoly, was well known to Great War enthusiasts, and particularly so to the Western Front Association members. Those who were lucky enough to be on Battlefield Tours when he was the acting guide would hear the story of the crucifix while gathered in the *Oak Dump, Spoil Bank* or *Chester Farm* Cemeteries or alongside the *Damm Strasse* outlining the account of the 47th [London] Division's action in the Battle of Messines.

Then again, while visiting different areas or just speaking on the coach, others may or may not have noticed that he was constantly playing with something on the chain around his neck? That something was his uncle Vincent's crucifix.

Much appreciated for his vast knowledge of the Great War and his willingness to share it with anyone and everyone, he spent every spare moment he had on the battlefields of France and Flanders, 'Spag' passed away peacefully on 5 October 2008 and was buried, wearing around his neck his uncle Vincent Sabini's crucifix. He will be missed but not forgotten by family, friends and acquaintances – and by literally hundreds of Great War enthusiasts.

Notes:

1. Although territorial units were attached to Regular Army battalions earlier in the war, the 2nd London Division (later the 47th [London] Division, was one of the first two Territorial Divisions to enter the fighting, the first being the North Midland Division (later the 46th Division).

2. In September 1915, at the Battle of Loos, a group of the London Irish, led by a Sergeant Edwards, then captain of the battalion's football team, kicked a ball across No-Man's Land towards the enemy. Despite intense enemy fire, the ball was finally kicked into the German trenches. In a desperate fight, the London Irish captured and held their objective. The football itself is now in the Regimental Museum and the memory of Sergeant Edwards feat is commemorated every year on Loos Sunday, the nearest Sunday to 25 September.

White Château

Like many châteaux constructed with white stone (a sure sign of wealth) in war-torn Belgium, the German occupied Palingbeek Château was given the nickname 'White Château' or 'White House' by British troops early in the Great War and, as with many troop-generated nicknames, White Château (the Germans named it Bayern Schloss) was adopted and made an 'official' map reference by the military cartographers.

In 1870 the château had been bought as a country home by the Mahieu family, a well established family dynasty in the textile industry from Armentières in Northern France,

When her husband Auguste Mahieu died in 1900, Mary Louise Ferry decided to make it the permanent residence for her and her two sons Auguste and Michel.

Between 1901 and 1903 it and its 60-hectare grounds were totally refurbished, being inaugurated with great ceremony in 1905 with festivities and events lasting for two weeks. A major feature of the refurbishment was a tree-lined road [a sunken road for the better part of its length] running directly from the château driveway entrance to the St. Eloi–Oosttaverne road, enabling the Mahieu family to avoid using the existing winding route of secondary roads, thus facilitating an easier trip to visit their other residence in Armentières. Severely damaged for obvious reasons by British artillery, this road became known to the mapmakers and troops as 'Damm Strasse'.

Palingbeek (White) Château before the war.

Overhead of the bombardment-battered White Château.

The Château and the Damm Strasse were totally destroyed during the war and never rebuilt. The old Château grounds now house the De Palingbeek Golf & Country Club golf course with its club house sited where once stood the Château itself. Remnants of the Château and a commemorative plaque are sited close by the clubhouse.

Evidence of the Damm Strasse making its way across the fields toward the St. Eloi-Oosttaverne road can still be seen from the road just outside where the drive way and entrance to the Château began.

The shell-damaged, German-held White Château in 1916.

The White Château closer to the opening of the Battle of Messines in 1917.

White Château after the Battle of Messines.

Photograph by Philip Woets.

Today, the Memorial Plague and remains of the battered stoneworks outside the golf course clubhouse now standing on the original site of White Chateau,

A LONDON IRISH CRUCIFIX AND WHITE CHATEAU

Madame Mahieu lost both of her sons during the war, both serving with the French forces, 28-year old Auguste as an infantry officer and Michel, aged 26 as a pilot,

As well as the small bluestone memorial commemorating the château and the two Mahieu sons just outside one of the entrances to today's golf course, another, featuring bronze statues of both Auguste and Michel in their military uniforms, is situated outside La Fréres Mahieu building in rue Jean-Jaurès, Armentières, France.

OP DEZE PLAATS STOND ER OOIT EEN MACHTIG KASTEEL, EIGENDOM VAN DE FAMILIE MAHIEU. TIJDENS DE EERSTE WERELDOORLOG WAS DIT KASTEEL DOOR DE BRITTEN GEKEND ALS "WHITE CHATEAU" EN DOOR DE DUITSERS ALS "DAS BAYERNSCHLOSS". HIER WERD ER TUSSEN 1914 EN 1918 VOORTDUREND GEVOCHTEN. VOORAL OP 7 JUNI 1917 TOEN LONDENSE TROEPEN VAN DE BRITSE 47STE DIVISIE DE PUINEN VAN HET GEBOUW UIT DE HANDEN VAN HET 61STE DUITSE REGIMENT VEROVERDEN. NA DE WAPENSTILSTAND WERD HET KASTEEL NOOIT HEROPGEBOUWD EN IN DE PLAATS KWAM HET BESCHEIDENER GEBOUW DAT NU ALS CLUBHUIS DIENT.

On this site once stood a magnificent Château belonging to the Mahieu family. During the First World War the Château was known by the British as White Château and the Germans as Bayern Château Under constant bombardment, it was totally destroyed during the opening barrages of the Battle of Messines in June 1917, On 7 June it was captured from the German 61st Regiment by the 47th (London) Division The Château was never rebuilt after the Armistice and on its site today stands a golf course clubhouse.

The Memorial Plaque [see photograph on previous page] and its English translation.

The bluestone memorial to the Mahieu brothers who fell in the Great War sited outside the golf course that was once part of the White Château grounds.

The Mahieu brothers memorial in rue Jean-Jaurès, Armentières, France.

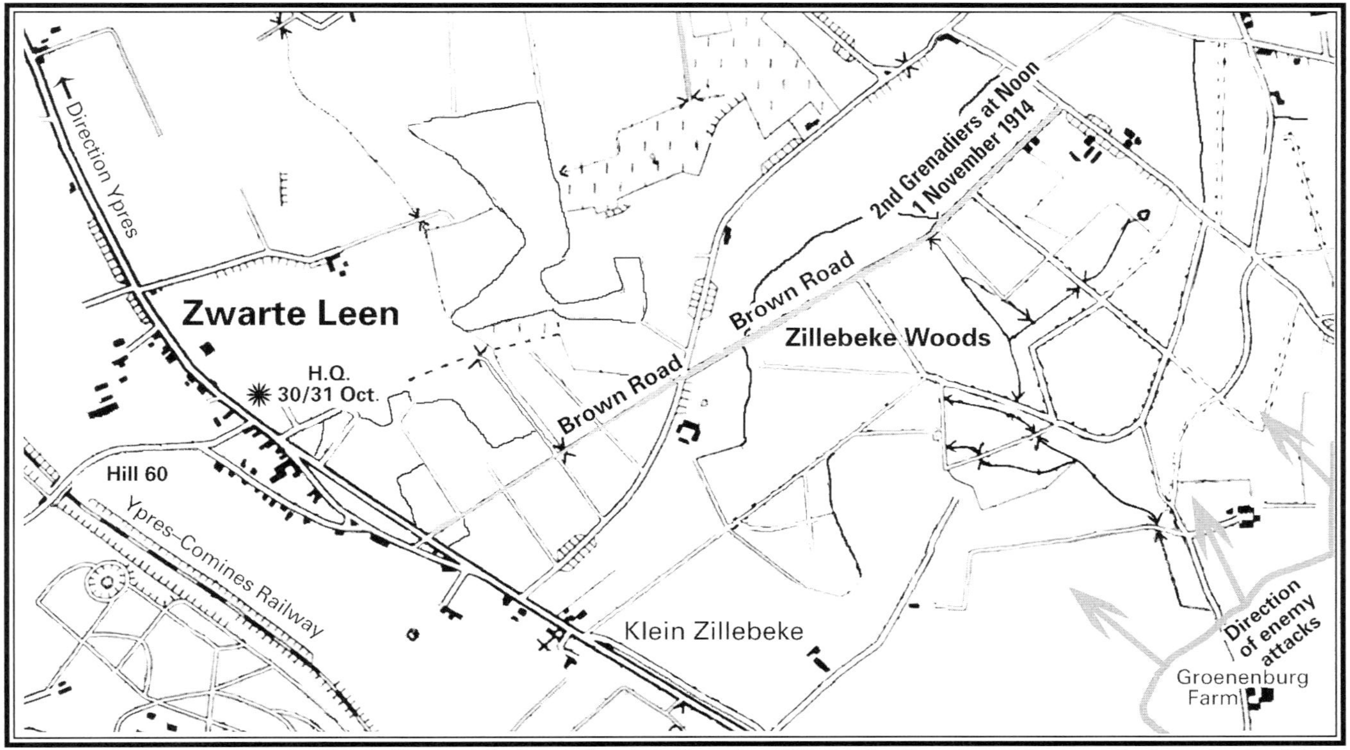

The Brown Road running through Zillebeke Woods. Defended at all costs in November 1914, it belies the nature of the tranquil, pleasant and well-kept ride running through the equally as pleasant woods of today.

Direction Ypres

Hill 60

Ypres-Comines Railway

Zwarte Leen

H.Q.
30/31 Oct.

Brown Road

Klein Zillebeke

Brown Road

Zillebeke Woods

2nd Grenadiers at Noon
1 November 1914

Direction
of enemy
attacks

Groenenburg
Farm

A persistent haze of gunsmoke all along the ride.
Grenadier Guardsman (Anon).

2
THE BROWN ROAD, ZILLEBEKE
2nd Battalion, The Grenadier Guards
Zillebeke, Ypres, October–November 1914

BROWN ROAD runs through the Klein-Zillebeke woods from a point south of *Greenjacket Ride*, toward Klein-Zillebeke itself.[1] Today it is either forgotten or unknown, and usually deserted. It does not figure highly on the itinerary of the Ypres Salient visitor, yet in November 1914 during the First Battle of Ypres it formed a fulcrum upon which the outcome of this vital battle was finely balanced.

On 30 October a dangerous situation developed due to a break in the line south of the Menin Road. The 2nd Grenadier Guards, 1st Irish Guards and 2nd Ox & Bucks were detached from the 2nd Division and moved south to Klein-Zillebeke to reinforce the cavalry north of Hollebeke Château. By 1.00 am on the 31st they were dug in between the Ypres-Comines railway and the Klein-Zillebeke road. They spent a long, wet night in their trenches, then a longer day of fighting, starting with heavy enemy shelling drenching the surrounding woods. In the afternoon Lord Cavan, C.O. 4th Guards Brigade, sent the following message:

> The situation is extremely critical. You are to hold your ground at all costs. Sir Douglas Haig relies on the Grenadiers to save the First Corps and possibly the Army.

44-year old Lieutenant-Colonel W. R. A. Smith C.M.G., commanding the Grenadiers placed every available man into the firing line from where they responded with a determination ingrained by several hundred years of duty, discipline and tradition, and they held their ground.[2]

On hearing of the outcome Lord Cavan, sent another message:

> Splendid. Hang on like grim death. You may yet save the Army.

They had proved their value earlier in the year on the heights above the River Aisne, and did sterling work in this battle for Ypres with the 2nd Division at Reutel and *Polygon Wood* – but it would be here in Zillebeke Woods that they would truly leave their mark.

Lieut.-Col. Smith C.O. 2nd Grenadier Guards.

With heavy shell-fire sweeping the whole locality they didn't give an inch, meeting the enemy advancing through the wood near the railway at about 3 pm with withering fire. The situation nevertheless remained critical when the Germans brought up field guns and plastered the Grenadiers' trenches until darkness eased the situation and the shelling finally stopped. The next morning the Grenadiers were faced with a scene that would be the norm for troops in future years. What had once been open farmland was now riddled with trenches ploughed up by shellfire, with the Groenenburg Farm complex facing them in total ruin.

Sir John French described the afternoon of 31 October 1914 as: "the most critical in the whole battle" as the British fought defensive actions all along the line against overwhelming odds. The 1st Somersets at Ploegsteert Wood under Major B. Prowse; the 1st London Scottish in action on the Messines Ridge, the 2nd Worcesters charge at Gheluvelt Château; the 7th Division battling to hold things together south of the Menin Road with its Royal Welch Fusiliers and Life Guards fighting to the last at Zandvoorde. These, and many other actions, contributed to a situation that the imperious Duke of Wellington, might have described as another 'close run thing'. But it wasn't over yet. On the night of the 31st the Grenadiers were relieved, retiring to Zwarte Leen where they thought they would get some rest. But it was not to be. Sir Douglas Haig had sent a message to Lord Cavan which was passed on to all regiments in the line:

> The German Emperor will arrive in the field today to conduct operations against the British Army The G.O.C. First Corps calls upon all ranks once more to repeat their magnificent efforts and to show him what British soldiers really are.

The enemy was now concentrating on smashing the trenches of the Irish Guards on the left of the line with high explosive shells, causing them to retire to the woods about 200 yards to the rear, Meanwhile the rest of line was being driven-in and a breakthrough was imminent.

The Grenadiers were ordered to leave all spare equipment in a farm to the rear of *Brown Road* and clear the wood southeast of it. With bayonets fixed they swept through, only to find that the enemy had left. However, their advance to the wood's edge enabled a reorganisation of the line.

2 November saw four attacks launched on the new line, but the Grenadiers, with steady fire and a firm commitment not to be moved, ensured they made no headway. Time and again their fire crackled through the trees repelling every onward rush from a determined enemy. Never once did they wilt, although the last attack at 5.54 pm, caused serious problems. The Germans advanced singing patriotic songs, blowing bugles and beating drums, hoping to intimidate the morale of the defenders, but the line was garrisoned by men of a unique metal, and the attack died away. In the morning, over 300 bodies of the enemy dead were found in front of the trenches.

This was the day the British Expeditionary Force held firm, and the Kaiser, waiting at his headquarters near Menin, began to realise that, for him, there would be no triumphal entry into Ypres. The B.E.F, described by a noted British historian as a 'thing of beauty', had drawn blood, exhausting the patience of the German Imperial Army which had planned such a campaign for years.[3] That depleted, never-to-be-the-same-again, 'Contemptible Little Army' had prevailed. But there was more to come for the troops at Klein-Zillebeke

Things were comparatively quiet following the evening attack of 2 November. It seemed the Germans had abandoned attempts to break the line here, but this was not so. As the morning mist cleared on the 6th, heavy shelling and infantry attacks were renewed with a vengeance causing such concern that another message was sent by

Today's Groenenburg Farm seen from the Zillebeke road with the woods in the background.

Lord Cavan to Lieut.-Col. Smith saying:

> Your position must be retained at all costs ... Redoubts must be occupied, every spare man and tool employed to make secondary trench. I trust you after splendid defence of last few days to maintain it to the end.

Early in the afternoon came the news that the trenches manned by Irish Guards had been driven-in and the Grenadiers' right was now in the air. Then came the news that the enemy had reached *Brown Road* and were advancing toward a gap to the right rear of the Grenadiers. Added to this was the toll exacted by German machine gun nests in the ruins of Groenenburg Farm. Lord Cavan called in the Household Cavalry, then in reserve at Sanctuary Wood, which galloped to within 500 yards of Brigade HQ, dismounted, and joined the fray. Soon Klein-Zillebeke was filled with troops from both sides engaged in close-quarter fighting. While this was going on a company of Grenadiers to the right of the line had been wiped out, almost everyone killed or wounded.

Again a message from Lord Cavan:

> Hang on tight to Brown Road. Try and get in touch with half battalion Sussex Regiment sent to farm at Irish Guards' H.Q,

With the help of well-sited machine guns and a number of stragglers collected from those left behind during the Irish Guards withdrawal, the Grenadiers plugged the gap for the remainder of the night, keeping in touch with the Sussex to the right and aided by the Ox & Bucks who kept sending up men from their reserves. By 4 o'clock in the morning they had consolidated a new line, extending it the full length of Brown Road.

From 7–9 November artillery and howitzer shelling continually damaging their trenches. The bombardments intensified on the 10th and part of the right of the line was thrown back, giving the Germans the opportunity to direct enfilade fire. The wood itself saw trees crashing down making communications between units virtually impossible. Casualties were rising with the fallen trees hindering the collection of the wounded. The bombardment became so intensive by midday that it seemed unlikely that anyone would survive. Mercifully the battalion went into Corps reserve on the night of the 10th, being relieved by the 2nd Munster Fusiliers and the Welsh Regiment, the relief taking the better part of the night because of the devastation in the wood. The 2nd Munsters, fresh out from its depot in Tralee, Southern Ireland, were to add to its reputation at Zillebeke Woods bringing assistance to the hard-pressed line with its own brand of Irish grit. Its effort was of great value, so much so, the children back in Cork were soon singing a street ditty of their own:

Oh the Kaiser Bill, tried so very hard,
when he lined our front with the Prussian Guard.
But the brave old Munsters still fought hard,
and held them back at Ypres.

The Grenadiers were now looking forward to a quiet four days of rest, but found instead they were to spend this 'rest period' marching about the line supporting various units – always accompanied by enemy shelling.

On the 11th they were detailed to support an attack to retake trenches captured by the Prussian Guard southwest of Polygon Wood and were to suffer heavy casualties while crossing open ground, and even more while lying out in the open awaiting orders. The attack was eventually abandoned and the battalion then received instructions to dig a new line of trenches near to the Menin Road.

On the 13th it move to *Sanctuary Wood*, taking more casualties then, in the middle of the night, the battalion was ordered back into the line with the 4th Brigade, its four days of 'rest' finally over.[4]

On the 15th the Grenadiers were back in the *Brown Road*, positioned either side of the Cavalry Brigade where they spent two quiet days before, on the 17th, the Germans made their last serious attack on Ypres. Heavy casualties were the order for that bitterly fought day but the Grenadiers again held fast, repulsing 12 attacks.

The German dead and wounded at the end of the morning attack was estimated as 1,200. By evening the attacks had died down and Lord Cavan at Brigade HQ in a private letter to the Officer Commanding the Grenadier Guards wrote:

I really should cry if the Germans got into Ypres before we go. On the 17th before the attack they threw over 200 big shells in and around my Headquarters and for one and a half hours it was pretty horrible, but the dug-outs saved us ,,,

The 18th and 19th saw more heavy shelling, but no infantry attacks and, on the 20th, the Grenadiers were finally relieved and marched off to St. Jean. From there they were to march to Ouderdom and then onto Meteren where they went into billets to refit, reorganise and rest.[5] The Grenadiers and fellow Irish Guards had been nothing short of magnificent while holding back the Germans at Zillebeke Woods, playing a valuable part at First Ypres. This was a defining battle in the course of the conflict and British troops, hard-pressed all along their line had been made aware of Sir Douglas Haig message to the effect:

For several days the battle seemed on a knife edge, but the defence of the Guards at Zillebeke even in face of mounting losses in officers and men was rock-like.

Today, the sector of the Brown Road held by the 2nd Grenadier Guards still runs through the woods at Klein-Zillebeke, but much quieter and in a different condition to that of 1914.

The battle frenzy during November began to wane, human endeavour could not maintain it. German attacks began to 'wither on the vine' and First Ypres concluded successfully for the British. The route to the Channel Ports was barred to the Kaiser's armies.

In his final letter to Lieutenant-Colonel Smith, on the night the Grenadiers left for Ouderdom, Lord Cavan noted something which, seemingly of no importance considering what the Grenadiers had experienced, reflects his pride in the discipline of those serving guardsmen, Grenadier and Irish alike.[6] He wrote:

The men have all kept up a respectable appearance which has been an example, considering that it has been impossible to change an article of clothing for four weeks. It is hoped that some officers and men may be able to get home for a few day's complete rest and change.

Zillebeke Woods and the *Brown Road* of today, the latter now a well kept public walkway through the woods, have slipped back into rural tranquillity. Nevertheless, today's visitor can easily make the leap back in time and give tribute to soldiers, friend and foe, who lie in unmarked graves over an area once so critical to the outcome of the First Battle of Ypres. They were doing their duty. May they rest easy.

Notes:

1. The Brown Road was named as such by British cartographers. Belgian ordnance maps of the time showed the ride coloured brown, indicating a metal layer-strengthened track for use by heavy agricultural vehicles and equipment.

2. Lieut.-Col. W. A. Smith CMCG was killed at the Battle of Festubert on 19 May 1915 and is buried in Le Touret Military Cemetery, Richebourg-L'Avoue, France.

3. In one of his lectures, the late military historian John Terraine referred to the B.E.F. of 1914 as a 'thing of beauty'.

4. For a time the battalion was answering to 4 different generals, receiving different orders from each of them due to units in the line being so hopelessly mixed up and constantly changing from one brigade to another.

5. The 2nd Grenadier Guards had moved into the Ypres area with a 3,700 strong muster of officers and men. When it left the line for its move into rest billets in Meteren on 20 November the battalion strength was about 2,000.

6. The Earl of Cavan was commissioned into the Grenadier Guards in 1855. He retired as Colonel but was recalled to command 4th (Guards) Brigade from September 1914 to June 1915. He then commanded, in succession, 50th Division, the Guards Division and 14 Corps at the Somme in 1916 and at the Battle of 3rd Ypres in 1917. He succeeded Sir Henry Wilson as Chief of the Imperial General Staff in February 1922, He died in August 1946, aged eighty.

That Old Army of England, wounded to the death,
held its dying arms outstretched across the way,
and against the nobility of that last stand nothing
could prevail.

Battle Book of Ypres, 1927.

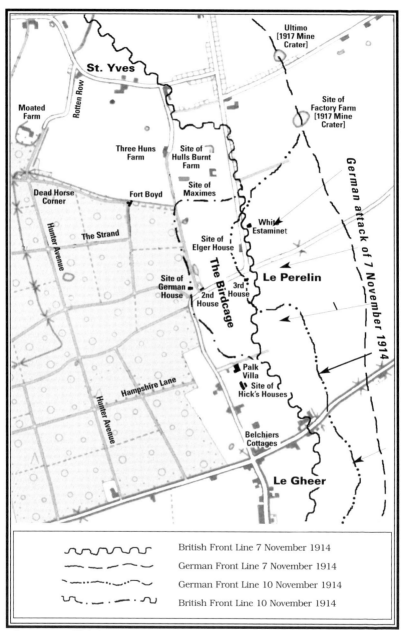

∿∿∿∿	British Front Line 7 November 1914
— — — —	German Front Line 7 November 1914
—·—··—·—·—	German Front Line 10 November 1914
∿·—·—·—·⌐∿	British Front Line 10 November 1914

After a series of failed counter-attacks to recapture the 3rd Worcesters trenches lost to the enemy on 7 November it was decided to accept the situation and consolidate the line caused by the breakthrough. The configuration of the resulting barbed-wire fortification shielding this salient in the British front caused troops to nickname it 'The Birdcage'.

It is only a complete absence of an enemy
that makes a soldier feel heroic.
Capt. P Cochrane.

3
BIRTH OF THE BIRDCAGE
The 3rd Battalion Worcestershire Regiment
and the 4th Division, Ploegsteert Wood 1914

OCTOBER AND NOVEMBER 1914 could be said to be the months that were to change the Great War on the Western Front from one of movement to entrenchment, and on to one of attrition. German attempts to outflank the Allied left had failed. Similarly the Allies were unable to turn the enemy's right wing and drive it back through Belgium. *The Race to the Sea* was over, the front establishing itself in a line that would remain, with little forward movement by either side, until the German offensive in April 1918.

The Battles of Armentières in Northern France and First Ypres in Belgian Flanders were fought – the British capturing Armentières, with the fighting closing down on 2 November, and First Ypres ending on the 22nd with the Germans failing to take the town, but occupying the high ground around it in a line arcing from north to south – the predecessor of what would become the infamous Ypres Salient.

On 31 October the enemy had attacked in force causing desperate battles to be fought along the length of the thinly held British line.[1] Although the action at Gheluvelt along the Menin Road east of Ypres was the most dramatic, the main assault was farther to the south, its objective: the occupation of high ground in the Wytschaete–Messines sector. Once it was taken, the enemy intent was to focus its pressure on the line between Messines in Belgium and Armentières in Northern France breaking through, then wrapping-up the allies by sweeping south to the rear of Armentières and northwest towards Kemmel, by-passing Ypres on its way to the Channel Ports, their ultimate objective. Massed German infantry supported by heavy artillery hammered the British line as far south as Frelinghien on the banks of the River Lys northeast of Armentières. A torrent of shells of all calibres crashed down on the British troops followed by wave after wave of infantry attacks in a determined effort to smash the line. The left of the line south of Ypres was held by the 2nd Cavalry Division around Messines with the centre and right of the line garrisoned by the 11th Brigade, 4th Division. When the Cavalry was eventually driven back, it left the line with a distinct indent running from St. Eloi to St. Yves, with Ploegsteert Wood (anglicised to 'Plugstreet' Wood by British troops) in the angle it formed where the right of this indent met with the remainder of the line.

On 1 November, the British 3rd Division was temporarily disbanded and one of its battalions, the 3rd Worcestershire Regiment, depleted in strength after the bruising it took from the fighting at La Bassée the month before, was detached from the division's 7th Brigade to support the 4th Division in holding this line.[2] The Worcesters joined the 4th's 11th Brigade just west of the village of Ploegsteert. From there its D Company was detached to support the 1st East Lancashire Regiment in trenches near the village of Le Gheer at the south-east corner of Ploegsteert Wood. Next day the rest of the battalion moved to positions at *Hill 63*, listening to enemy gunfire apparently arriving from all directions. staying for the rest of the day until, as evening fell, and with its D Company back from support duties, it moved into the line, relieving the 1st Hampshire Regiment in trenches east of the wood.

Then followed four days in a bleak, shell-torn landscape dotted with the ruins of farms and their outbuildings; all destroyed in the bombardments of the previous week. Their English names – *Moated Farm, Huns Burnt Farm, Elgar House, White Estaminet, German House* and others, given to them by the troops, belied their actual condition – no more than piles of rubble acting as map references.[3]

These four days saw the battalion's troops huddled in shallow, water-logged trenches taking rifle and shell-fire from which it suffered casualties of one officer and 22 other ranks wounded and 9 killed.

On 6 November a blanket of thick fog cut observation to less than 50 yards. Enemy fire increased in intensity, and the defending Worcesters could do little more than fire blindly at intervals into the fog, straining their eyes and ears alike in anticipation of an attack, knowing the Germans were likely to use the fog to screen a breakthrough. Evening fell and, with darkness adding to their plight, their ability to see anything was now totally obscured. Shelling continued to batter the front from St. Yves to Le Touquet when, between 3 and 4 am on the morning of the 7th, heavy shellfire hammered the trenches and, at about 5 am, what they had expected happened – the enemy, Saxon troops of the 19th Corps' 106th and 34th Regiments, launched a massed, infantry attack along the whole sector. The line held, except for the section between Le Gheer and St. Yves which had taken the brunt of the attack. Le Gheer fell, with the enemy sweeping through the fog, overrunning two company's of Worcesters' in their trenches just north of the village. Although resisting stubbornly, nothing they could do stopped the German onrush penetrating some 600 yards into the wood. The two Worcester companies in the support trenches aided by a company each from the 2nd Inniskillings and the 1st Seaforth Highlanders managed to stop the advance but could do nothing to regain the lost trenches. A hastily set up counter-attack launched at 8 pm that evening by the 1st East Lancs, 2nd Lancashire Fusiliers, 1st Hampshires and the Inniskilling Fusiliers drove the enemy out of Le Gheer and from about 300 yards of the trench running northward from it along the wood's edge. Dense fog prevented any form of British observation, troop co-ordination or artillery support. and no headway was made in the Worcesters' sector. They were unable to get near, let alone recapture their lost trenches. Throughout the night of 7-8 November the Worcesters desperately hung on to the line to which they had been forced to retire and were finally relieved on the evening of the 8th by the Seaforth Highlanders, moving to billets around *Butler's House*, a farm west of the wood.[4]

Just after midday on the 8th, another attack by the East Lancs to recover the trenches was unsuccessful, although the attackers did get to within 50 yards of them before being forced back to about 200 yards in front of their original start line.

Yet another attack was launched on the night of the 9-10th, this time with troops from the 2nd Lancashire Fusiliers with a company of East Lancs in support, but again enemy machine gun and rifle fire caused its failure. Following this last attack it was decided that no further attempts would be made to retake the lost trenches. Orders were issued to consolidate the line, an area which ran about 500 yards from north to south and 250 yards from east to west. The nature of these

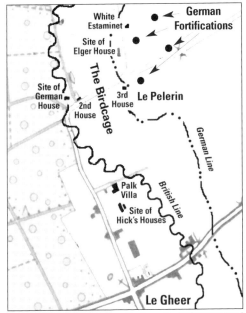

The situation following the attack on the 3rd Worcesters' trenches on 7 November. The lost trenches were never retaken and the Germans proceeded to construct four heavy fortifications behind the Birdcage (under which mines were tunnelled by the British [but never triggered] in preparation for the Battle of Messines).

barbed wire fortifications caused troops to nickname it *The Birdcage*, an area remaining in German hands until September 1918 when they withdrew during the allied advance.

During the period of these later attacks the Worcesters were at rest in Bailleul. They served a few more short stints in the line before, on the night of 16-17 November the battalion was relieved and marched to billets in Petit Pont, a village northwest of Ploegsteert. In its 16-day period at the front it had taken casualties of 4 officers and 51 other ranks killed, 3 officers and 143 wounded and 35 missing. Most of the fallen are commemorated on the Menin Gate and Ploegsteert memorials, their bodies never recovered. So ended the battalion's brief sojourn in Ploegsteert Wood, their lost trenches marking the western edge of the *Birdcage* for the rest of the war.[5]

The situation in and around the wood for the rest of the month and into December was one of static trench warfare with intermittent shelling and accurate sniping causing daily casualties to the battalions in the line. Later in December orders were received to set up a diversionary action for the French Army's attack on Arras, thus holding the German forces in the Ploegsteert area, preventing their transfer south to be used against the French. This action was to:

> ... demonstrate and seize any favourable opportunity to capture any enemy's trenches on their front.

Later modified to:

> ... attacking some point of the enemy's line with the object of preventing him from moving his reserves to meet the French attack.

The 4th Division's raid targets were the enemy trenches (the 3rd Worcesters' trenches of the month before) and a number of houses between Le Gheer and St. Yves east of the wood:

> ... limited in its scope to driving the enemy from the salient in his line and readjusting the line now held by the 4th Division.

This "... salient in his line" was in fact the *Birdcage* – seemingly the powers-that-be had changed their minds on: "... no further attempts would be made to retake the lost trenches".

The attack launched at 2.30 pm on 19 December against 'The German House Defences', three ruined houses in the *Birdcage* named *German House* and *Second* and *Third German House*, all used by the enemy for observation and sniping. The plan was to capture and put them in a state of defence and consolidate the ground.

Meanwhile the French action at Arras was abandoned, but it was decided to go ahead with 'readjusting the line' as, according to High Command, it would result in a tactical gain.

The 1st Rifle Brigade were to advance astride the road running east then north from German House to take the enemy trenches 300 yards east of the wood. The 1st Somerset Light Infantry to its left would overrun the fortifications on its front, and the 1st Hampshire Regiment on the right would "swing its left forward to conform with the advance, when it was completed."

Accurate artillery support for the attack was doomed to failure from the start as the guns were unable to register on the houses and trenches in the *Birdcage*, these being sheltered by the trees of Ploegsteert Wood itself and, as it was, artillery shells at that time were limited to 4 to 6 rounds per gun per day. Because of this small calibre howitzers were to support the attack, while the destroying of enemy

German House.

wire and covering fire for the troops was left to machine guns and an Austrian mountain gun brought up from ia farm south of the River Warnave (aptly named *Mountain Gun Farm*).[6] Another drawback was the state of the ground – the damage caused by shelling and the wet weather had left it knee-deep in cloying mud and slush, potted with slime-filled shellholes and littered with boughs, branches and foliage from the damaged trees.

From 1.30 to 2.30 pm British guns shelled the German lines, but every shell fell short, with shrapnel frequently bursting over the Somersets' line. The howitzer shelling rarely reached east of the Le Gheer–St. Yves road and the Austrian mountain gun on the eastern edge of the wood which was to destroy the enemy wire and demolish German House, destroyed the house, but had no effect on the wire.

The attack launched at 2.30 pm saw the 1st Rifle Brigade troops instantly faced with concentrated rifle and machine gun fire, immediately killing the officer in command. They succeeded only in capturing *German House* and *Second German House*.

On the left, mud, shell holes and a combination of enemy fire and British artillery 'shorts' from their rear, quickly brought the Somersets to a standstill. The enemy line was roughly 120 yards away but it was 4 pm before the Somersets managed to battle their way past the track parallel to the Le Gheer-St Yves road, only to find the position was untenable.

On the right the Hampshires were held up just beyond *Second German House* and, about 5 pm, supports were called up to link left of the Rifle Brigade, resulting in a firing line running from the 1st Hampshires' trench through *Second German House* to the wood's edge in front of the Somerset Light Infantry's trench. Beyond this it was impossible for any advance due to lack of covering fire and the shell-pitted state of the ground. A trench was dug inside the edge of the wood and garrisoned before the rest of the attackers retired to the *Hunter Avenue* support line. *German House* was fortified and kept within the new line and the attack was called off. Although not meeting its full objectives, it had driven the enemy out of the wood, and moved the British line to the edge of it. Work began immediately on turning the new line from a hastily dug, water and slime-filled shallow trench into breastworks, but consistent gunfire and sniping caused this job to run well into 1915 before it was finished.

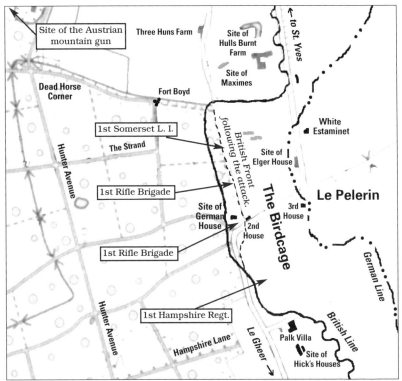

The attack on 19 December resulted in the capture of German House, Second German House and the clearing of the enemy from the wood. Second German House was eventually abandoned when the attack-force retired to the Hunter Avenue support line,

Following this attack, no more attempts were made to take the *Birdcage*, nor did the Germans try to eject the British from the wood until 1918. The *Birdcage* remained intact, adding to its toll of casualties over 200 officers and men across the three battalions involved in the raid. One of those casualties was young Reuben Barnett, a 15-year old Rifleman with the 1st Rifle Brigade. His body, like many others, was only recovered during the 1914 Christmas Truce. He is buried in Plot IV, Row E, Grave 10 at Rifle House Cemetery within the wood together with others of his battalion who died in the raid. The 1st Somerset Light Infantrys' casualties lie in Plots I and II in Ploegsteert Wood Military Cemetery, also within the wood, and those of the 1st Hampshires rest in Plots I and II of Lancashire Cottage Cemetery on the Ploegsteert–Le Gheer road.

During the 1914 Christmas Truce, British and German troops mingled together both north and east of Ploegsteert Wood but there is no record to suggest that gatherings took place within the Birdcage. At one time, the Germans proposed to a Rifle Brigade stretcher-bearer a 'formal' collection of the British dead who had fallen close to and behind their lines, but the Rifle Brigade did not have the authority to meet their conditions, namely that the Germans would collect the bodies and carry them to British stretcher-bearers and that the artillery of both sides were to hold fire from 10 am to 2 pm 'German time'. Bodies of the British dead in No-Man's Land east of the wood were still being found by raiding parties in 1916 but, due to enemy alertness and the generally impassable state of the marshy ground, it proved impossible to bring them back to the British lines for burial.

From early 1915 onward, small raiding actions by both sides were always a threat, serving to keep troops on either side of the *Birdcage* alert at all times, while sniping became almost an art form. Apart from this raiding, sniping, regular shelling and a deal of tunnelling and small mine blowing, the area was considered a quiet, 'cushy' place to serve with both sides using it to train incoming units, acclimatising them into the 'whys and wherefores' of trench life, and teaching them the necessary life-preserving techniques of static warfare.

The *Birdcage* developed a different type of 'notoriety' when a breastworked-ride, named the *Tourist Line* running south from Fort Boyd was considered a line safe enough for visiting dignitaries to see the front for themselves from behind a section of the breastwork named *Tourist Peep* – and in broad daylight too.[7]

Amongst those known to have made such a visit were General Allenby, Admiral Sir Lewis Bayley, Lieutenant-General Robert Baden-Powell, Major-General Sir Reginald Pole Carew, and a few Japanese and Russian officers.

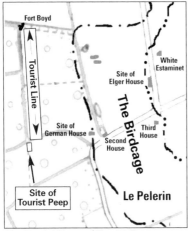

The Tourist Line and Tourist Peep.

In early 1917 the area became a hive of activity when both New Zealand and Australian engineers constructed dressing stations at Charing Cross and Underhill Farm, in preparation for the for the outset of the Battle of Messines when eight of the Australian 3rd Division's attack battalions would eventually move through and around the wood from camps in the Romarin and the Le Bizet areas.

Four mines tunnelled below the Birdcage by the 171st Australian Tunnelling Company, were to herald the assault's opening but, because of their close proximity to the German trenches they were never blown, being considered too far right of the shoulder of the Messines Ridge and the German main defensive trench system. Also, the Germans were more adept at reaching, occupying and fortifying mine craters, and the close proximity of the lines in this sector could well have given them a strong advantage for enfilade attacks on the Australian troops during the assault if they had occupied the craters.

One of these four mines was triggered during a storm in 1955, but the other three still lie dormant below this old strongpoint. Ploegsteert may not yet have heard (literally) the last of the *Birdcage*.

A German's eye view of Ploegsteert Wood from across the Birdcage today, the photograph taken from the position of a German strongpoint. The house on the left behind the telegraph pole is built on the site of Third German House.

Notes.

1. The attack on 31 October saw the first time the Germans used their new weapon, the Minenwerfer, against British forces.

2. The 3rd Division lost 219 officers and 5,616 other ranks between 12 and 31 October. The 7th Brigade alone was reduced to under 1,900 men, the 3rd Worcesters suffering more than 300 casualties including 18 officers.

3. Such names were selected to enable troops to identify strongpoints, dressing stations, observation posts, supply dumps, camps, roads, tracks, woodlands and mustering points all along the Western Front. It was decided that these points of reference, developed and used by the troops, should become 'officialised' and they began to appear on military trench maps from 1915 onward.

4. Obviously named by a London Regiment, this area became known as Charing Cross due to its proximity to the start of the Strand Communication Trench which ran from west to east through the wood – the Strand in London starting at Charing Cross just southeast of Trafalgar Square.

5. The battalion re-joined the 3rd Division as part of its 8th Brigade at Neuve Eglise before, on 19 November, moving into billets north of Kemmel as reserve to the 2nd Cavalry Division.

6. The Austrian mountain gun was sited for its part in the attack on the northern edge of Ploegsteert Wood just west of Moated Farm. After the attack it was returned to its original site – in a haystack at the aptly named Mountain Gun Farm edging the River Warnave south of the Ploegsteert to Le Gheer road.

7. The *Tourist Peep* barricade section was sited at the point the track leading from Rifle House intersected with *Tourist Line*, presumably the most convenient and safest point from which to view the Birdcage.

A British view of the The Birdcage today, the photograph taken roadside from the site of German House. The house on the left is on the site of First German House with that seen between the two telegraph poles on the right being on the site of Third German House.

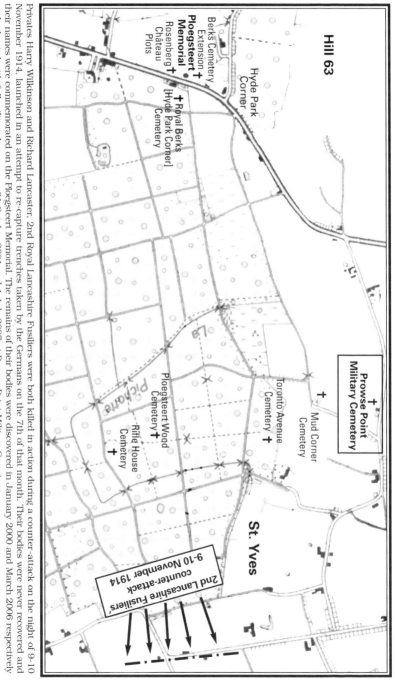

Privates Harry Wilkinson and Richard Lancaster, 2nd Royal Lancashire Fusiliers were both killed in action during a counter-attack on the night of 9-10 November 1914, launched in an attempt to re-capture trenches taken by the Germans on the 7th of that month. Their bodies were never recovered and their names were commemorated on the Ploegsteert Memorial. The remains of their bodies were discovered in January 2000 and March 2006 respectively and reburied with full military honours on 31 October 2001 and 4 July 2007 at Prowse Point Military Cemetery.

And where the earth was soft for flowers we made a grave for him that he might better rest.
A Soldier's Grave – Francis Ledwidge,

4
FUSILIER GRAVES
Privates Harry Wilkinson and Richard Lancaster,
2nd Battalion, the Royal Lancashire Fusiliers.
Ploegsteert 9-10 November 1914

THE NIGHT OF 9-10 NOVEMBER 1914 saw the last counter-attack delivered against the German occupied front and support trenches behind the *Birdcage*, a fortified area breaking the British front line on the eastern side of Ploegsteert Wood. This section of the British front, manned by two companies of the 3rd Battalion Worcestershire Regiment, had been overrun following heavy German artillery and ferocious infantry attacks in the early morning of a foggy 7 November.

As with the two previous attacks attempting to recover the lost trenches on 7 and 8 November respectively, this one ended in failure.[1] The British attack had managed to break through the front line of trenches, had taken the *Elger House* complex of buildings and entered sections of the German-held trenches but, enfiladed by well directed machine gun and rifle fire, the buildings and trenches had to be abandoned and the attacking troops withdrawn. The war diary of one of the battalions involved in the attack on the night of 9-10 November, the 2nd Battalion Royal Lancashire Fusiliers supporting the 2nd Argyll & Sutherland Highlanders, records casualties of one officer and 15 other ranks wounded and two other ranks killed.

One of the two Lancashire Fusiliers killed was 29-year old Private 8850, Harold Wilkinson from Bury in Lancashire. On 20 August 1914, this former fire-beater in a local Bury cotton mill, landed at Boulogne, France with his battalion as part of the 12th Brigade, 4th Division, leaving behind him at home in Lord Street, Bury his pregnant wife Eva and their 6-year old son Harry.

His wife and young son would not see him again, nor would he ever see his unborn child, a daughter to be named Florence. The last they heard from him was on a postcard he had sent from Ploegsteert stating "May God be with you until we meet again" They would never know what had happened to him other than what very little information could be gleaned from the official War Office telegram they would have received giving notice of his death.

He had experienced and survived the ferocious fighting with the battle-weary 4th Division from August through October at Cambrai, the Marne, the Aisne, Le Cateau and Armentières only to be cut down on a cold Autumn morning in a shell-holed, slimy, mud-ridden stretch of land on the edge of a wood in an action that had little or no chance of success from its outset – a counter-attack against an entrenched, better-equipped, superior-in-numbers enemy who were expecting and prepared for such an action.

His body was never recovered and after the war his name was commemorated on Panel 4 of the Ploegsteert Memorial, at Hyde Park Corner, one of the 11,447 names of officers and men who fell and who have no known grave on this memorial to the missing in southern Belgium, just north of Ploegsteert village on the left of the road to Messines.

The site of Private Wilkinson's death, then a stretch of muddy, shell-torn land, now an area of cultivated farmland, is almost exactly opposite the spot where the Memorial stands, separated only by the leafy mass of Ploegsteert Wood – the wood in which he was serving at the time of his death.

Time passed and Eva, who never remarried, came to terms with life without her husband, and both the son Harry and daughter Florence grew up without a father. A sad but familiar story experienced by thousands of families during the war and post war periods.

Private Harold Wilkinson, 2nd Battalion, Royal Lancashire Fusiliers

The Ploegsteert Memorial on the left hand side of the Ploegsteert-Messines road.

Pte. H. Wilkinson's name commemorated on Panel 4 of the Ploegsteert Memorial.

On 3 January 2000, 86-years and 3-months later, a discovery on the old battle area of that unsuccessful counter-attack just north of the *Birdcage* would spark an event which would eventually bring together the descendants of Private Harry Wilkinson's extended family, some of whom over the years, had lost contact with each other.

The then 39-year old Patrick Roelens, a sharp-eyed member of the local community, working with the Warneton Historical Society was researching the area just north of the site of the old wartime *Birdcage* at the same time as a farmer was ploughing a field for the first time, a part of his land that had been used for pasture since the end of the war. Roelens noticed something in one of the newly turned furrows which turned out to be an identity disc together with what appeared to be finger bones. Stamped into the disc were the figures and words '8850 H Wilkinson CE LF'.

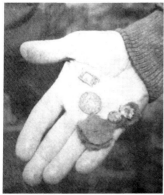

Items found with Harry Wilkinson's remains.

The dog tag which led to the confirmation of Harry's identity and prompted the search for his relatives.

With the farmers permission he roped-off the area and carefully excavated to a depth just below topsoil level and discovered the skeletal remains of a soldier with an apparent head wound. There was no trace of weaponry or ammunition and the position of the soldier was such that he was lying on his left side with his head seemingly resting on his arm, and his left leg bent beneath his right. The remains of a pipe was lying close to the skull, and a bottle was found alongside the body together with a Lancashire Fusiliers' shoulder metal, a coin, a few fragments of khaki cloth and a crude, handmade triangular piece of metal that could have been used as a tool, maybe for scraping off mud or something to that effect.

From the depth the remains were found, just below the level of the ploughshare, together with their configuration it seemed unlikely that he was buried. The lack of a rifle and/or bayonet, no small arms ammunition, the pipe and the bottle would indicate that he was wounded, made comfortable by his comrades and left behind in the general withdrawal from *Elger House* with a view to being collected later, or with the hope that the enemy would collect and care for him as a prisoner. It was quite normal at that time in the war, to collect weapons and ammunition from those wounded and dead on the battlefield.

During the Christmas Truce of 1914, troops from by both sides collected the dead who had fallen in the vicious fighting in this sector during the previous 3 months. Shelling and the morass-like state of the ground could well have been the cause of the Harry Wilkinson's body being covered weeks before the truce took place, the snow during this period adding to the chances that it would not have been seen. As it was, those buried would have been recorded, but the subject can only bring with it conjecture and what actually happened to this lone Lancashire Fusilier will never be known.

The remains were collected, reported to the Belgian Ministry of the Interior and then delivered to the British authorities where the Ministry of Defence set about the task of authenticating that the soldier's remains were that of Private Harry Wilkinson. An extensive search for any surviving members of the family was instigated through the Royal Regiment of Fusiliers, with invaluable aid from the local Manchester and Bury press. His were the first remains to be found and identified in Belgium for 20 years

The Commonwealth War Graves Commission began its work in determining military cemetery in which Fusilier Wilkinson would be

The original marker produced and placed by Patrick Roelens above the spot where Private Harry Wilkinson's remains were discovered. Ploegsteert Wood can be seen in the background.

The memorials that now only identify the field, not the site, in which Private Wilkinson's remains were discovered. They are positioned on the edge of the field to enable the farmer to continue, unimpeded, with the cultivation of his field.

buried and put in hand the preparation of a military headstone. The date of the burial, 31 October 2001, coincided with a ceremony marking the 25,000th sounding of *Last Post* at the Menin Gate in Ypres.[2] The chosen cemetery was Prowse Point Military Cemetery, just north of Ploegsteert Wood, about a quarter of a mile away from the spot where Harry Wilkinson lost his life 87-years previously. He would be buried with full military honours, with ceremonial duties being the responsibility of the 1st Battalion Royal Regiment of Fusiliers.[3]

Six Fusilier pallbearers carried the coffin into the cemetery against a backdrop of music from the Minden Band, Queen's Division. They removed the Union Flag, a wreath of poppies and a Fusilier beret with its red and white hackle, from the coffin in preparation for its lowering into the grave. With the lowering completed another six men of the battalion fired 3 shots over the grave.

The ceremony, attended by the Duke of Kent and other dignitaries, was conducted by the Regimental Padre Mark Moreton and Chaplain Ray Jones of St George's Memorial Church in Ypres.[4] Nine members, making up four generations, of Private Wilkinson's family were present to see him buried, ranging from his 59-year old granddaughter, who was 3 years old when her grandmother Eva died; his 51 year old great-grand-daughter, whose mother was the

Members of the Royal Regiment of Fusiliers' pallbearing party undergoing last minute rehearsal before the ceremony began.

The Duke of Kent arriving at the cemetery together with other dignitaries for Harry Wilkinson's burial ceremony.

The Minden Band, Queen's Division muster in preparation for the burial ceremony.

Pallbearers of the 1st Battalion Royal Regiment of Fusiliers carry the coffin to its resting place.

A Fusilier pallbearer placing a folded Union Flag on Private Wilkinson's coffin before its for burial.

daughter he never saw, and his 9-year old great-great grandson, proudly wearing Private Wilkinson's campaign medals. The ceremony was crowned by the Sergeant in charge of the burial party marching to the grave and dropping the yellow hackle of the Lancashire Fusiliers to lie with the coffin in perpetuity. At the close, the folded Union Flag and poppy wreath taken from the coffin were presented to his granddaughter.

Members of Private Wilkinson's family attend the ceremony.

A final touch to funeral occurred when the writer was stopped by a late-arriving Belgian journalist on the road from the cemetery to the Ploegsteert-Messines road. He wanted to know why so much importance had been attached to the ceremony and why it was so 'special'? At the time the Lieutenant-Colonel and Class 1 Warrent Officer of the Royal Regiment of Fusiliers were passing us on the road. It was suggested to the journalist that he ask the question of one of them, which he did. The Warrant Officer fixed the journalist with a not-too-friendly stare, answering simply: "Because he was a Fusilier", and continued walking up the road with his Lieutenant-Colonel.

Private Wilkinson's burial ceremony continues with the pallbearing party lowering his coffin into place in Grave 7, Row A of Plot I in Prowse Point Military Cemetery, Ploegsteert, Belgium.

The Duke of Kent pays his respects before gardeners of the Commonwealth War Graves Commission placed the military headstone and completed the grave.

Richard Lancaster photographed with his son, also named Richard, in the early 1900s.

Five years later, in March 2006, the remains of three soldier were discovered by French amateur archaeologists Emmanuel Bril and Frederic Seynave in the same area as were those of Private Wilkinson.

One of the soldiers was identified as another Lancashire Fusilier, Private 8372 Richard Lancaster who fell during the same counter-attack as Harry Wilkinson,

Artifacts found with Private Lancaster's remains were his bayonet scabbard, cap badge, shoulder metals, ammunition pouches, toothbrush, razor, fork and spoon, and his metal dog tag, the artefact prompting the investigation into authenticating his identification. He was buried with full military honours at Prowse Point Military Cemetery, the same as that of Private Wilkinson, on 4 July 2007, the Honour Guard and Buglers of the 1st Battalion The Royal Regiment of Fusiliers from Celle, Germany providing the Ceremonial Party.

31-years old when he died, Richard Lancaster, was born in Preston, Lancashire in 1883 and, at 18-years old, had enlisted in March 1901 at Bury, serving 3 years with the colours [he was stationed in India during the Boer War] and 9 years as a reservist before being called

Private Richard Lancaster's dog tag bearing his number 8372, and his reconditioned cap badge and shoulder metals.

Photographs on this page by Andy Mackay.

The Honour Guard, Pallbearers and Buglers of the 1st Battalion, Royal Regiment of Fusiliers together with the Reverend who conducted the ceremony.

Private R Lancaster's coffin being lowered into the grave,

9 members of Pte. R Lancaster's extended family in front of Panel 4 of the Ploegsteert Memorial on which his name is commemorated

back to the colours again at the outbreak of the Great War in 1914. Married to Phoebe Porter, he was the father of four.[5] His son Richard (pictured with his father on the previous page), was seven-years old when his father died and, having fought in the Second World War, was to live to his 72nd year before passing away in 2001. Two of Lancaster's granddaughters were traced, sisters Myra Webster and Doreen Grimshaw (daughters of William, another of Lancaster's sons, (just 4-years old when his father died] as was a great-grandson John Hoban whose mother Barbara, a third granddaughter, died in 2002. Altogether, nine members of the surviving extended family attended the burial together with 300 other attendees including contingents from the Belgian Navy.

Artifacts belonging to Private Lancaster were handed to granddaughter Myra Webster at the end of the ceremony

Private Harry Wilkinson's grave at Prowse Point Military Cemetery, 31 October 2001.

Private Richard Lancaster's grave between those of the two unidentified soldiers whose remains were discovered at the same time as his, 4 July 2007.

46

A document entitled *2nd Battalion. List of Places of Burial of Officers, N.C.O.'s and Men of the above Battalion who have been Killed in Action or Died from Wounds* indicates that 17 N.C.O.s and Other Ranks of the Lancashire Fusiliers were buried east of Ploegsteert between 2-14 November 1914.[7]

Of these the place of burial of 15 are noted as: *"Behind the trenches at Ploegsteert"*; one *"At the edge of Ploegsteert Wood, St. Yves"* and one *"Behind the trenches at St. Yves"*. Five of these casualties are listed as having died on 10 November, the final day of the counter-attack. In the same document Private Wilkinson was listed as buried *"Behind the trenches at Ploegsteert"* and Private Lancaster *"Behind the trenches at St. Yves"*.[8]

This would indicate that 3 others of the 2nd Battalion, Privates S, Brown [No.9468], W. Robinson [No.8394] and J. Sheridan [No,9129], casualties of the counter-attack, still lie at rest in the area.[8]

Notes:

1. One of those who fell in the first counter-attack of 7 November, Sergeant John [Jack] Barnes of the 1st East Lancashire Regiment, was shot in the temple while leading his men in the bayonet charge. His brother Octamus, serving in the same Regiment, informed the family that his elder brother, one of the six brothers who fought in the Great War, had fallen too close to the enemy-held trench to be recovered. According to Jack's Commanding Officer, Lieut.-Col. Lawrence, his body was buried in a plot in the field with other officers and men who died in the attack. A search in 1917 by the then Imperial War Graves Commission, could not find the grave in the badly shell-damaged burial plot. Sergeant Jack Barnes' name is commemorated on the Ploegsteert Memorial.

Sgt. J. Barnes.
1st East Lancs.

2. As part of the anniversary, a different soldier, sailor or airman killed in the Great War was honoured each day of 2001. At this 25,000th sounding of Last Post at the Menin Gate on the evening he was buried (attended by the Duke of Edinburgh), Private Harry Wilkinson was the first to be honoured.

3. The Royal Regiment of Fusiliers was formed on 23 April 1968 from four infantry regiments:– The Lancashire Fusiliers, The Royal Northumberland Fusiliers, The Royal Warwickshire Fusiliers and The Royal Fusiliers (City of London Regiment).

4. The Duke of Kent is President of the Commonwealth War Graves Commission as well as Colonel-in-Chief of the Royal Regiment of Fusiliers.

5. Private Lancaster's wife, passed away in the 70s at the age of 103.

6. The names of all 17 Fusiliers [including those of Privates H Wilkinson and R Lancaster] are commemorated on Panel 4 of the Ploegsteert Memorial.

7. St. Yves was a small hamlet just northeast of Ploegsteert Wood and the lost trenches. Totally destroyed during the early October 1914 bombardments, it was never rebuilt. It is sometimes confused with hamlet of St. Yvon which developed after the war on the northwestern corner of Ploegsteert Wood.

8. The remains of two unidentified soldiers found at the same time as Private Lancaster were buried either side of him during the same ceremony.

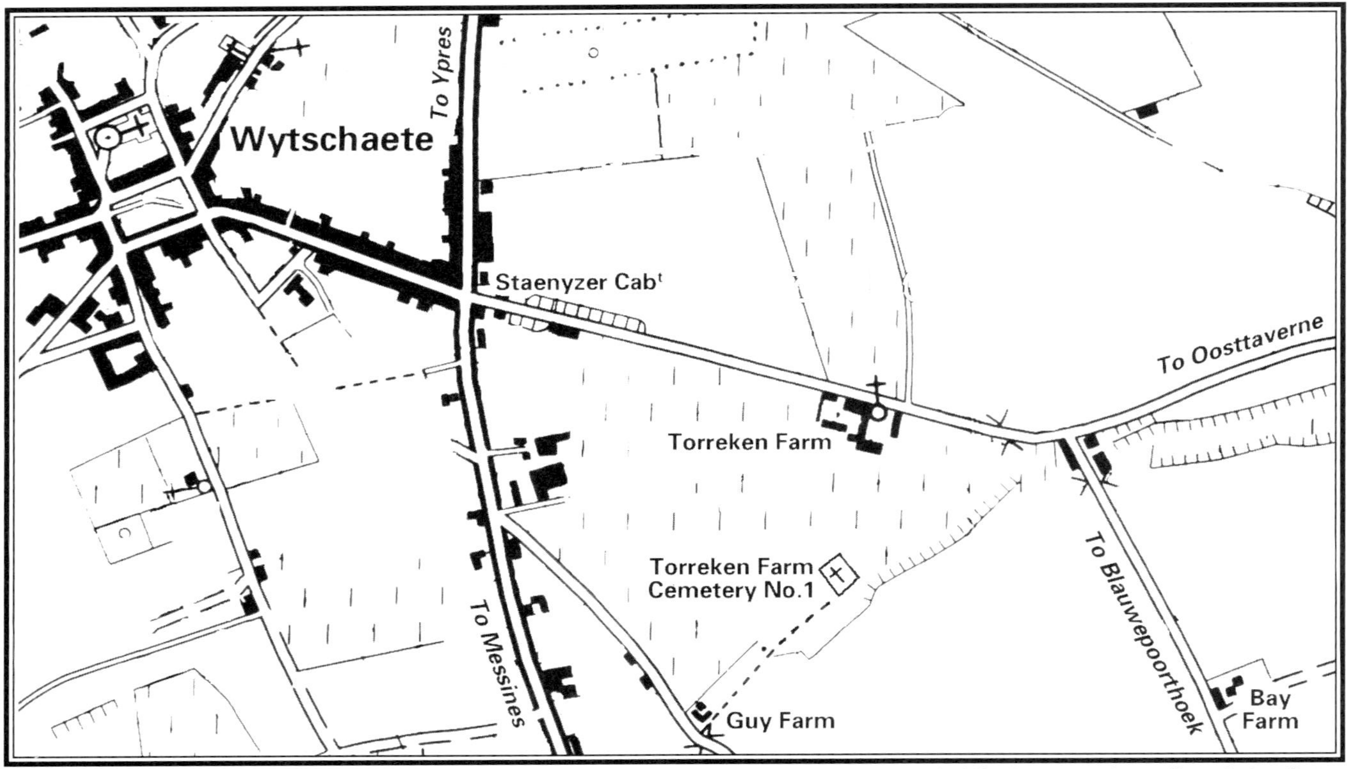
Wytschaete
To Ypres
Staenyzer Cab^t
To Oosttaverne
Torreken Farm
Torreken Farm
Cemetery No.1
To Messines
To Blauwepoorthoek
Guy Farm
Bay
Farm

Torreken Farm Cemetery No. 1, sharing the open pasture land with a German underground shelter. Slightly difficult to get to, but well worth the effort.

He flies in other skies. Another Universe to see.
Tony Spagnoly.

5
AVIATORS AT TORREKEN FARM
2nd-Lieutenants Paul J Rodocanachi and Norman L Watt R.F.C.
Torreken Farm, Messines Ridge, 27 July 1917

NOT EVERY BRITISH FLYER cruising the skies over the Western Front in the antiquated 'flying machines' which passed for fighting aircraft at the time was destined to become a household name like 'Aces' of the calibre of a Mick Mannock, Albert Ball or Jimmy McCudden. Many were doomed to die unknown and unheralded after only brief periods of training and air time. This was especially true in the April of 1917, which went into aviation history as 'Bloody April', when the enemy held the ascendancy of planes and pilots, spearheaded by Baron Manfred Von Richtofen. The Red Baron was making his mark above the trenches, outwitting the British pilots flying in their cumbersome planes, the German models being superior in manoeuvrability, armament and speed. It was a critical time for the British Air Service until planes like the Nieuport Spad, SE5 and SE5A were available to bring some sort of parity in the skies.

Baron Manfred Von Richtofen.

Oscar Boelcke

Until then, under-trained British pilots with a minimum of flying hours in their log books were so much 'fodder' for the likes of Von Richtofen and his scout squadrons. His attack techniques, conceived by his mentor Oscar Boelcke and now honed to perfection, were downing British pilots in machines inferior to his Fokker D1s at an alarming rate, and particularly so those acting with duties of artillery spotting, ariel photography and intelligence gathering. Planes might be affordable but the aviators, even with their lack of training, were not. The life expectancy of a subaltern in the trenches was two to three weeks, but those of a pilot was considerably less, especially so with those on reconnaissance duties. Theirs was a different war, totally removed from the slime and obscenity to be found below, but flying without the comforting thought of being in formation with other planes, pursuing the same task. The low altitude flying plane, the pilot and the observer himself, sitting behind the pilot, concentrating on the land below, were little more than sitting ducks for the likes of Baron Von Richtofen's high flyers, their only means of defence being the pilot's sharp eyes and the observer's Lewis Gun – machine speed and manoeuvrability not being available options.

For the fighter pilots it was equally as dangerous, but at least that's what they were up there for – trained, fully equipped and in custom-built aeroplanes which, although often inferior, didn't stop them looking for a fight. Their existence was one of short sharp bursts of pulsating excitement, laced with long periods of quiet, almost boring patrolling, then a return, if the fates decreed, to warm, comfortable surroundings, a meal in the mess with their peers, a good night's rest until wakened by a servant at dawn to prepare for another early patrol. But theirs could be a lonely, violent death, often without the comfort of a Christian burial with their colleagues in attendance, especially if they were shot down over enemy territory.

Thousands of British pilots met their untimely deaths during those dramatic war years as the British Air Service developed at an alarming rate to keep pace with the requirements of the vast armies in raging battle below. Some would exceed that grim maxim of lasting barely two to three weeks on active service, but many would not.

On 27 July 1917 two young aviators, 2nd-Lieutenants Paul John Rodocanachi and Norman Lindsay Watt, were to fit that grim profile, thudding into the ground at the western end of the Messines Ridge

Fokker D1s of the type flown by Baron Manfred Von Richtofen and his squadron – the infamous 'Red Baron' and his 'Flying Circus'.

near the village of Wytschaete in a sector only recently wrested from the enemy following the Messines offensive of June 1917.

Paul John Rodocanachi was born in Calcutta in August 1898 where his father was engaged in Anglo-Indian business. Pictures from the period show him to be a tall youth with almost Italianate good looks. As the years advanced a classic English public school education beckoned, and he attended Rugby.

He was 16-years old at the outbreak of the Great War, a war which was to have such dire repercussions for so many of his generation. Imbued with the wave of patriotism sweeping the country at the time, he had had no other option than to wait patiently until he was 18-years old and able to present himself for military service. Steeped in the military lore of the cadet militia which all students at Rugby were immersed, it was the new air service which interested him and when his time came to enlist, he was granted a commission in the Royal Naval Air Service.

In March 1917 he began basic training at Vendome near Paris in a Caudron trainer in which he cut his 'flying teeth'. He made his first solo flight on 17 March 1917, only weeks after joining the service and, with less than two hours of dual flying instruction, seemed to have little difficulty in mastering the basics.

Rodocanachi advanced quickly to the more sophisticated Curtis (IN.4), then to the larger Armstrong Whitworth in which he completed his main training at Cramlington in Northumberland. This was on 7 May 1917 after he had trained in air photography and a stint of night

The Caudron G III, first flown on reconnaissance missions early in the war, was later used primarily as a training aircraft.

flying with 58 Squadron. He had just over 30-hours of solo flying noted in his log book, and had been in the service eight weeks, but things were moving apace for him.

His last weeks in the U.K. were used to further his training before spending a brief posting to Scrampton.[1]

On 11 June 1917 he made his first acquaintance with the RE8, built at the Royal Aircraft Factory, Farnborough and much used by the Royal Flying Corps on the Western Front in support and observation duty.[2] Rodocanachi found this aeroplane. a 'difficult animal' to master, and once landed at the wrong airstrip by mistake. This error of judgement wasn't unique to him; Britain's leading 'Ace', Jimmy McCudden V.C., was to commit the same error in France in July 1918, an error which certainly contributed to his death.

Rodocanachi was to make many landing mistakes while mastering his cumbersome machine before his superiors considered him ready to play his part in the great affair. Pilots were in extremely urgent

The Armstrong Whitworth, larger and more robust than the Curtis.

The RE8, stable in flight but cumbersome and lacking in speed and manoeuvrability.

demand due to the British advances at Arras in April 1917, the fall of Vimy Ridge, and victory at the Battle of Messines in June of the same year. The ground forces were in desperate need of as much air support as they could get in their need in ranging for 'artillery shoots' and observation as they inched across the plain of Douai.

On 5 July 1917, barely 16 weeks after joining the service, and just short of his 19th birthday, he left for France to join the Royal Flying Corps' 53 Squadron, then operating from an air base at Bailleul near Armentières in Northern France.[3]

They had an intensive introduction to the many duties that 53 Squadron was called upon to perform over the Franco/Belgian border sector between Armentières and Messines. Preparations for the opening of the 'The Battles for Passchendaele' (Third Ypres) were finalising, and nothing could be done to hide from enemy observers the movements of men and materials preparing for the 31 July launching of this massive offensive. Activity in the air by both German and British was becoming frantic.

Rodocanachi's log book recorded:

7 July, 5.30 a.m. – Weather too dud for shoot, so patrolled district.
21 July, 4.10 p.m. – Shoot 283 very good – engine vibrating.
24 July, 4.25 p.m. – Shoot 151. Weather very bad, shot at 2 pairs of Huns.
25th July, 5.40 – Shoot with 151. Visibility good, just missed tree tops.

He noted 15 'shoots' between 5th and 25th July, but that entry for the 25th was to be the last he would record. On 27 July, just 2 days later and 20 days after entering the fray, 2nd-Lieutenant Rodocanachi and his observer 2nd-Lieutenant Norman L. Watt were to experience a violent end when their RE8 was hit by a burst of cannon-fire from an enemy aircraft.

While flying an artillery-ranging exercise over the lines near Ploegsteert Wood, a German scout plane on the lookout for such prey attacked.[1] Its bullets ripped through the RE8's flimsy structure killing Rodocanachi and leaving Watt to take over the controls, a complicated and difficult task in itself due to the crowded configuration of the cockpit with pilot and observer sitting back-to-back in its confined space. The plane was well into enemy territory before Watt was able to turn and make his way back to the British line. But his courageous efforts were to no avail. The RE8 spun into an uncontrollable dive, flattened-out in an apparent attempt to land, but then crashed into a large shell hole in a field alongside Torreken Farm just east of the Wytschaete-Messines road.

2nd-Lieut. Watt, although alive when dragged from the wreckage, later died of his wounds.

The area was garrisoned by men of the 13th Rifle Brigade at the time and, as the evening light began to wane, its chaplain, Captain Chamberlain, conducted the burial ceremony of the two aviators in a small nearby burial plot.[4]

As with so many other pilots during the Great War, so ended the lives of two young men, a short, active life and service encompassed in a scarcity of detail: birth, education, military service and then death.

Ironically, the tragic scene was witnessed by Norman Watt's brother, Lieutenant W. E. Watt, also a member of the Royal Flying Corps, who was flying in the neighbourhood.

On 1 August he wrote to Rodocanachi's family:

Dear Mr. Rodocanachi,

I am writing to you because I think you will be glad to hear of anything in connection with your nephew's death, and I will be able to tell you more than anyone else, as I saw the whole thing from the air and afterwards got details from the ground, as your nephew's observer, at the time, was my brother, N. L. Watt. They were up ranging a 12" Howitzer battery on the afternoon of the 27th. At 3:40 p.m. a Hun scout made an attack on the machine I was in and then made off for home. After going about a mile away from us we saw him dive down on another of our machines. He got to within 100 yards and after firing for a little went off. I don't think our machine opened fire at all. It looked as if the observer had his attention fixed on the target he was watching, and the top plane prevented the pilot from seeing the Hun approaching. After the fight our machine, which was at 6,000 ft, flew very uncertainly straight across into Hun land. It looked as if the pilot was killed or badly wounded and that the observer was trying to fly the bus. Eventually the machine turned back and wobbled towards our front line. Then it fell in a spin, quite out of control. Near the ground it flattened out and seemed to be going to land safely, but crashed into a huge shell hole and was badly smashed. They fell about 800 yards behind our front line and it was not two days later before I was able to see the man who pulled him out of the machine. He told me the pilot was dead and had probably died of bullet wounds in the air before crashing. The observer was unconscious and died within a few minutes, so we will never know any more details. They were buried side by side by the chaplain of the 13th Battalion Rifle Brigade in a little cemetery about 700 yards east of Wytschaete]. I have taken a couple of photos of the graves and will let you have some copies and also a map showing the position of the cemetery when I come home in a week or two, for we are not allowed to send these things through the post. I have also arranged for a permanent cross, made from a propeller, to be put up, so there is no chance of the spot being lost.

There is no need for me to tell you how much I sympathize [sic] with you, but I feel sure they are both happy and glad to know that their bodies are lying in the ground we took from the Germans last month.

Yours very sincerely,

W. E. Watt

So the short careers as military aviators of both Paul John Rodocanachi and Norman Lindsay Watt came to an end on the Messines Ridge. They filled precisely the sombre framework of two to three weeks service before their demise, the same fate of so many others at that time.

To pay tribute at their graves in a tranquil grazing field a little off the beaten track at Wytschaete in Belgian Flanders is a humbling experience in itself. At rest with many of those who fought and died in the trenches below them, just another two lives lost on a mild summer evening all those years ago.

May they rest in peace

Notes:

1. During the Second World War, RAF Scrampton Airfield in Lincolnshire was home to Squadron X – 'The Dambusters' – under Wing Commander Guy Penrose Gibson VC, DFC, DSO 1 bar.

2. The RE8 - RE stood for Reconnaissance Experimental - was introduced into the Royal Flying Corps service in 1916. It became one of the most widely used aircraft for reconnaissance, observation and artillery-spotting. Although extremely stable in flight, its poor manoeuvrability and low speed made it an easy target for enemy fighters. The aeroplane was not very popular with the air-crews because of its tendency to spin, which caused many accidents, fatal and otherwise, It was nicknamed 'Harry Tate' after a well-known Music Hall artiste of that time.

Royal Flying Corps personnel attending to the graves of lost colleagues showing the typical propeller marker cross adopted by air forces of both sides during the war.

RE8

Built by: Royal Aircraft Factory, Farnborough.

Wingspan: 42ft. 7 ins.

Length and Weight: 27ft. 10ins. 4,109lbs. [loaded].

Crew: Pilot and Observer.

Armament: 303 Lewis Machine Gun.

Maximum Speed and Ceiling: 102mph. and 13,000ft.

Power: 150hp. RAF 1A

3. The Bailleul Airfield from where Rodocanachi and Watt flew their last mission with 53 Squadron was sited near the Bailleul Communal Cemetery, in company with an important railhead and hospital centre.

4. 2nd-Lieuts. Rodocanachi and Watt are in good company at the CWGC Torreken Farm Cemetery No.1, where 88 UK and Australian troops also lie at rest. The 2nd Lieutenants are buried in Graves C6 and C5 respectively. The cemetery was started in June 1917 by men of the 5th Battalion, Dorsetshire Regiment as the burial plot for the small aid post sited here. In the field outside the cemetery walls a section of raised broken ground hides the remnants of the entrance to an underground German dugout, shelter or possibly one of their aid stations. Partly buried over the passage of time it can be identified by a short section of a ventilation shaft protruding from the ground. A closer inspection reveals the partly covered entrance (see photos below).

The partly concealed German dugout outside the walls of Torreken Farm Cemetery No.1 as it was to be seen in the 60s and 70s.

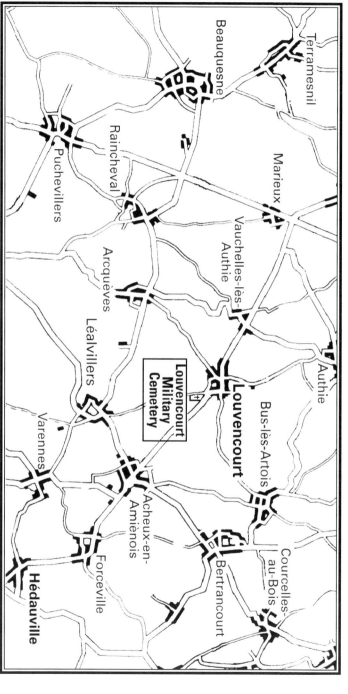

The scattering of agricultural villages around Louvencourt on the road from Doullens to Albert where Roland Leighton is buried in the local British Military Cemetery. Hédauville village further along the same road inspired his poem of the same name. He served with the 1st/7th Worcesters in the Ploegsteert area from April to June 1915. His poem, *Villanelle*, written for his mother, was inspired from the growth of violets in the north eastern part of the wood. Just before leaving the sector, he wrote the poem *Ploegsteert*, the last stanza of which almost foretells his death which occurred just 6 months later when he was injured and later died of his wounds in a Casualty Clearing Station at Louvencourt on 23rd December 1915.

58

Destiny has more resources than the most imaginative composer of fiction.
R. A. Leighton 1915, Hedauville.

6
A POET FOR PLUGSTREET
Lieutenant Roland Aubrey Leighton
1st/7th Battalion Worcestershire Regiment
Killed in Action 23 December 1915

WHEN LIEUTENANT ROLAND AUBREY LEIGHTON, 1st/7th Battalion Worcestershire Regiment, wrote his enduring words in the summer of 1915 about the 'Long white road that ribboned down the hill' in his classic verse, *Hedauville*, he could hardly have imagined that years afterwards, when the guns were silent, he would still be in this locality at rest in a soldier's grave, and that his former love and fiancée Vera Brittain visiting the battlefields with a companion in 1933, and still struggling with the grief of his loss, would recognise that defining landmark of the winding road as she passed through Hédauville on the way to his grave at Louvencourt Military Cemetery.[1] She had remarked:

> As the car lurched drunkenly between the yawning shell-holes I looked back, and it seemed to me that perhaps in November 1915, this half-obliterated track had still retained enough character and dignity to remind Roland of the moorland road near Buxton where we had walked one spring evening before the war ...

This must have been an emotional jolt to her as she remembered the future life they had contemplated together. Another broken dream.

Vera Brittain was not a stranger to grief, having lost so many close friends during the war years. Besides her fiancée, her brother Acting Captain Edward H. Brittain M.C. Attached, 11th Battalion Sherwood Foresters (Nottinghamshire and Derbyshire Regiment) had been killed in action on 15 June 1918 in the mountains of Northern Italy when several British Divisions went to that front to bolster the sagging Italian defences against the Austrian/German invader. His loss, so late in the war, had been a devastating blow to her family.[2]

Roland Leighton's battalion, a Territorial unit, was part of the 48th (Midland) Division which had served around the Ploegsteert Wood area, south of Ypres for indoctrination in the lore and life of the trenches, patrolling, raiding and holding a sector in close proximity to an enemy, sometimes only 100 to 200 metres away. Always a prolific letter writer, Leighton also found an outlet in verse, and his poetry and letters from Ploegsteert Wood in the April of 1915 gained him a reputation, and enraptured his sweetheart Vera, back in England.

His early life seems to have followed the usual pattern for boys of his middle-class background, living in comfortable affluence. Born in March 1895, that tragic year that seems to have borne so many of that doomed generation who died on the battlefields of Europe 20 years later, he certainly had the writer's genes within him as both of his parents were professional authors of some note. His father, Robert Leighton, the Postmaster of Merton College, Oxford, was also a noted literary critic of his day.

Roland trod the well-worn path to the British public school, with his student days spent at Uppingham College in middle England. Many of the close friends he made there were to join him on the list of the fallen in the conflict which was looming on the political horizon.

One of his close friends at school was Vera Brittain's brother Edward who, like so many others of his generation was also fated to die during the war. In July 1913, Leighton, through his friendship with Edward, was to meet Vera at a garden party following a Speech Day at Uppingham, and were attracted to each other on sight. Vera was preparing for entrance exams to Oxford University at the time and, with Roland and Edward both due to leave Uppingham for Oxford in July 1914, all three looked forward to being together for a long time in the foreseeable future.

In August 1914, Roland and Edward were at an Officer training camp which disbanded immediately war broke out.

As with so many of the young men of society at the time, both joined the general euphoria of patriotism that beset the country, delayed their further education at Oxford and volunteered for military service.

Due to their both being members of the O.T.C. members at Uppingham, they were granted early commissions. Roland, whose poor eyesight was overcome by a certificate from a family doctor who was persuaded not to mention it, joined the Norfolk Regiment, and Edward the 11th (Service) Battalion, The Sherwood Foresters. In the October of the year Vera went to Somerville College, Oxford and wasn't to meet with Roland again until the Christmas Holiday. While at home recovering from a bout of flu she received a letter from the university telling her that

Roland Leighton in the uniform of the Uppingham College Officer Training Corps.

Roland had transferred to the 1st/7th Worcestershire Regiment and was shortly leaving for France.

The regiment left on 31 March 1915 as part of the 144th Brigade, 48th (Midland) Division. From Boulogne the battalion, with its sister battalion, the 1st/8th, entrained for Cassel where the division was being concentrated and from where, on 5 April, it marched the 20 odd miles to billets in Bailleul. After 5 days of training the battalions then went forward to an area near Armentières for practical instruction and acclimatisation into trench warfare. The 1st/7th Battalion was attached to the 18th Brigade and the 1st/8th to the 19th from where their platoons were attached in succession to companies of the battalions in the line. Here they learned their trade and were initiated into the routine of trench warfare although, apart from odd enemy sniping and bombing together with not too frequent raiding, there was little warlike activity.

The division was then assigned a definite section of the front line between the River Warnave and the Wulverghem–Messines Road, covering Ploegsteert Wood and its environs. Lieutenant Roland Leighton, with his battalion now back with the 144th Brigade, went into the trenches of the right sector of the Divisional line where the Worcesters relieved the London Rifle Brigade. Casualties were on a low, if consistent, level in this part of the line, a sector generally seen as 'quiet' compared to others. That unique experience of the 1914 Christmas Truce had taken place along this part of the front, and Ploegsteert Wood maintained a general mystique and ambience all of its own, as the many writers and poets who had served there observed and fully documented with their writings.

Vera would not be left out of the general excitement and, seeing her brother and fiancee go off to war, she offered herself for war work.

Although against her family's approval, she volunteered for the harsh environment of military nursing and, on 27 June 1915, became a VAD (Voluntary Aid Detachment Nurse) which saw her working first at the Devonshire Hospital in Buxton, then at the 1st London General Hospital and later in France and Malta. Of her brother Edward, her lover Roland and herself, she would be the only one to return.[3]

Leighton in the meantime had became accustomed to his new form of life at the front, frequently putting pen to paper and sending his thoughts and observations in a

Vera Brittain in her V.A.D. uniform.

A photograph taken by Roland Leighton in Ploegsteert Wood in 1915 – possibly taken from the right hand side near the southern entrance of Hunter

stream of letters and verse both to Vera and his family in England. Life within Ploegsteert Wood captivated him, as the creative side of his spirit generated some meaningful verse which must have delighted Vera and his family, particularly his mother.

He was impressed by the sight of men living in dwellings in among the tree, tending plots of flower and vegetables, ducking intermittently as spent bullets and shrapnel from an enemy just outside the eastern fringe of the wood whizzed erratically about. The profusion of wild flowers and the delicate blue violets growing all over the battalion area must have enchanted him, and the soldiers carefully tending the graves of fallen comrades was a sight that would remain with him during his short life, On 25 April 1915 he had sent Vera some of those violets and, having been touched somewhat by the finding of the body of a British soldier killed in some earlier fire-fight and now partly submerged in the mud, he was compelled to put to paper one of the most enduring of his works, and sent it to his mother, forever associating Roland Leighton with 'Plugstreet' Wood:

Villanelle

Violets from Plugstreet Wood –
Sweet I send you oversea
It is strange they should be so blue –
Blue, when his soaked blood was red
For they grew around his head –
It is strange they should be so blue
Violets from Plugstreet Wood –
Think what they have meant to me
Life and hope and love and you
And you did not see them grow
Where his mangled body lay
Hiding horror from the day –
Sweetest, it was better so
Violets from oversea –
To you dear forgetting land
There, I send in memory –
Knowing you will understand.

He wrote to Vera in April 1915, who notes in her journal:

He says he has not been afraid, although he has been now under fire! His is afraid of his imagination, afraid of being afraid – so am I. That is why he in the midst of actual dangers, fears and dreads nothing, while I far away from all the signs of active warfare, shudder and tremble.

Another occasion touched her heart when he wrote that he had seen the grave of a dead German near his dugout, commenting with compassion: "Somebody once loved the man lying there."

Other pieces of verse flowed from Roland's pen during the period he spent in and around Ploegsteert Wood, which in turn would join his catalogue of works with *Villanelle* and the later *Hedauville* to be read and enjoyed by many down the years. He and Vera had become officially engaged on one of his leaves, so they were a very happy couple, planning their future once he had played his part in the war and had returned to civilian life. There was no reason for them to think otherwise. His service life until that time had not seen him face the dangers that others were experiencing in the Ypres sector farther north. His posting at Ploegsteert kept him away from the desperate battles of Second Ypres in the April of that year, and the battalion's eventual move south saw him miss the actions at Hooge and Bellewaarde in July and September respectively.

However, Roland's sojourn in and about wood was coming to an end. On 15 June the 144th Brigade withdrew into Divisional Reserve, then moved back into the left of the Divisional line between St Yves and the River Douve for another four day stint before learning that the 48th Division was about to leave the Ploegsteert sector, moving south to join the First Army in Northern France.

Just before the division left on 27 June, Roland wrote a piece which seemed full of his reluctance to leave a place he had grown so fond of; and with his destiny about to catch up with him, it also seems to touch upon his own mortality.

Ploegsteert

Love have I known, and dawn and gold of day time,
And winds and songs and all the joys that are,
And known once, and as a child that tires with playtime,
Leaped from them to the elemental dust of war.

I have seen blood and death, but all has ending,
And even horror is but made to cease.
I am sickened with love that lives only for lending,
And all the loathsome pettiness of peace.

Give me, God of battles, a field of death,
A hill of fire, a strong man's agony.

For Lieutenant Roland Leighton, the 'Poet of Plugstreet', 'a field of death, a hill of fire' would soon be his.

The Division arrived at its destination in the IV Corps area at Burbure on 1 July where the Worcesters' 1st/7th and 1st/8th Battalions went into reserve before moving with the rest of the 48th Division on 12 July to relieve the 47th Division at Les Brebis. From here Roland, with the 1st/7th Battalion was detached from the Brigade and sent on to Maroc, an unattractive mining area in

Northern France, a district vastly different to the pleasant surrounds of Ploegsteert Wood. They set about constructing reserve line defences before receiving counter-orders – the 48th Division was to join the newly formed Third Army in a part of the battle-front in France which was unfamiliar to British troops – the open country of Picardy around the River Somme. Leaving on the night of 16/17 July they marched the 17 miles back to Burbure, spending two days in billets there before entraining to join VII Corps north of the river. This was another 'quiet' sector of the battle line for Roland Leighton to enjoy and maybe to write about. The frontage for the British was from the river to Heburtine on the left running northward from the river at Corbie, past Albert over the undulating country studded with little villages whose names would become embedded in the minds of British troops in the following year and forever in the annuls of British military history.

The 144th Brigade went into reserve before moving into the front line on 30 July where they stayed until 7 August before being relieved and moved into billets, the 1st/7th Battalion finding comfortable quarters in the village of St Leger. They remained in this area throughout the Autumn, billeting by shifts in the surrounding villages of Courcelles, Souastre and Bus. This sector was 'quiet' during the summer and Autumn months and even 'quieter' during the winter, but driving rain and heavy frosts caused the battalions excessive work repairing the crumbling clay trench sides. This work alone made it impractical, virtually impossible, to consider any sort of aggressive action against the enemy. So far in his wartime experience Roland

Portraits exchanged between Roland Leighton and Vera Brittain in 1914.

had not experienced many of the dangers of trench warfare although troop movements, constructing defence lines and repairing damaged trench works had added a deal of knowledge to the other side of his military life. The training the Division was undergoing was in preparation for the planned Somme Offensive in July of the following year and the area it was manning was the focal point of the coming British attack. It must have been while serving in this area that Roland would have passed through or visited the village of Hedauville, and put his thoughts to paper in form of his verse.

Two items of news received by Vera just before Christmas 1915 were to excite and devastate her respectively. The first in a short letter from Roland on 17 December delighted her as it contained the information:

Leave from Dec. 24th–31st. Land on Christmas Day.

Her fiancée was due home on Christmas Day for a seven-day leave, the first time she would have seen him again since his last short leave in August when, on a train from London to Buxton, he had proposed marriage. One can only imagine the excitement the news of Roland's coming home for Christmas caused the Brittain household at Buxton. The happiness to be enjoyed in those seven days; the festive season to spend together walking the hills, planning a future, perhaps tenuous at the time, but to be talked about all the same.

Although Roland did not arrive at the scheduled time, Vera was not unduly worried as wartime travelling for soldiers to and from the front could not be expected to run like clockwork, nor did it. However, she was not at all prepared for the second piece of information in that fateful December of 1915. On the 27th she received the news via a telephone call from Clare Leighton, Roland's sister, that the family had received a telegram, the content of which, in stark and tragic contrast to Roland's short note read:

T223. Regret to inform you that Lieut. R. A. Leighton 7th Worcesters died of wounds December 23rd. Lord Kitchener sends his sympathy. *Colonel of Territorial Force, Records, Warwick.*

He had been wounded and had died of his wounds at a Casualty Clearing Station the night he should have been on his way home to be with her in England. It transpired that he had taken a wiring party out late on the night of 22-23 December to repair the wire defences at a spot known locally as 'Z Hedge' near Gommecourt Wood.

This area of the front in 1915 was considered 'quiet' during the summer, and even quieter during the winter. Due to the heavy frosts and torrential rain taking their damaging toll on the clay sides of the trenches of both sides at that time, all ranks found themselves working incessantly on repairing the trenches to keep their lines up to the expected defensive standard. Although attempting offensive action by either side was considered impracticable, intermittent shelling and other forms of aggression were ever present.

On the night of 23 December, either fixed enemy rifle fire trained on 'Z Hedge', or an alert sniper anticipating such nocturnal activity as the wiring party were undertaking, selected his target in the bright moonlight of the night, and Lieutenant Roland A. Leighton, the Poet of Plugstreet, fell, mortally wounded.[4]

He was taken to a Casualty Clearing Station at Louvencourt almost 10 miles away but severe shock had set in from his wounds, and he could not be saved. Fortified by the rites of the Church applied by a Roman Catholic Padre, he died peacefully around 11 pm on the night of the 23rd. He was buried on Boxing Day, Sunday, 26 December in the British burial plot sited just outside the village (today's Louvencourt Military Cemetery), where he rests in peace to this day. His Colonel, in his letter to the Leighton family, said the committal was carried out in bright sunshine to herald his passing.

Roland Leighton had experienced a defining moment in his life a few weeks before his death. Like so many thoughtful men in the trenches living in such close proximity to the regular death of others and the possibility of death to themselves, an entry into a 'new dimension' of life was as they saw it. He pondered deeply on such things and found he was veering back to the old faith in conflict with his sincerely held Anglican belief, finding the rock solid basic tenets, held by the Roman Church for the past two thousand years, offered him the strength he demanded in the continually dangerous existence he was forced to lead and, after applying for a short instruction by the Roman Catholic padres in the trenches, he was officially received into the Roman Catholic Church where he hoped he would find the solace he quested.

This news must have been quite momentous for both his and Vera's families for whom the Anglican Church was home. He would not be the only one to make this gigantic leap. He would be in the good company of a literary giant of the period, Siegfried Sassoon, Royal Welsh Fusiliers, who would make the same spiritual journey to Rome in the post war years, brought about through his experiences in the trenches. It is recorded that when Siegfried Sassoon was asked his views about the 'life eternal', he responded that if there is a life after death you will happily find his spirit wandering freely around Bois Français the small wooded plantation set above the village of Mametz on the Somme, where he recorded the attack on Fricourt as: "a sunlit picture of hell" on that bloody morning of 1 July 1916.

To have ventured the same question to Roland Leighton would probably elicited a similar response, possibly that he could be found

Perhaps
(To Roland Aubrey Leighton)

Perhaps some day the sun will shine again,
And I shall see that still the skies are blue,
And feel once more I do not live in vain,
Although bereft of You.

Perhaps the golden meadows at my feet
Will make the sunny hours of spring seem gay,
And I shall find the white May-blossoms sweet,
Though You have passed away.

Perhaps the summer woods will shimmer bright,
And crimson roses once again be fair,
And autumn harvest fields a rich delight,
Although You are not there.

But though kind Time may many joys renew,
There is one greatest joy I shall not know
Again, because my heart for loss of You
Was broken, long ago.

Vera Brittain

wandering among the quiet glades of Ploegsteert Wood where the stately trees conspire in the breeze to conjure up the eternal meaning of this mystical place, where the poet of Plugstreet seemed so content.
Notes

1. Roland Leighton is buried in Louvencourt Military Cemetery, France. Plot 1, Row B, Grave 20. His headstone gives his age as 19 but he was 21-years old at the time of his death. Vera Brittain visited his grave in 1921 and again in 1933 when visiting the battlefields of the Great War, In Thiepval she stood beside the British Memorial to the Missing saying this was one of the horrifying results of 'my generation's pursuit of heroism'.

2. Capt. E H Brittain, MC is buried in Plot 1, Row B, Grave 1 in Granezza British Cemetery, west of Venice, Italy.

3. On finishing her studies at Oxford Vera Brittain married in 1925 and had two children John and Shirley. She became a novelist and journalist and an active member of the Peace Pledge Union. Author of 29 books, her poignant memories of Roland, her brother and friends are expressed in the book *Testament of Youth*. She died on 29 March 1970. Daughter Shirley Wiliams became a forceful and prominent politician with the Liberal and the Liberal Democrats Parties and eventually became Baroness Williams of Crosby.

4. Vera received differing accounts of Roland's fatal wounding. The regiment's Colonel Harman spoke of fire from fixed rifles trained on the spot Roland was inspecting which his wiring party was due to repair and Roland's servant, who was with him at the time of his being wounded, spoke of a single shot from a sniper.

Violets still in Plugstreet
(A tribute to Roland Aubrey Leighton)

How quiet the mystical wood appears at this time of day
The towering trees conspire in whispers, but in the softest way
Tranquil is the perfect word to sum up this matchless mood
Can heavens halls compare at all with this glorious interlude?

Tread softly stranger at the Toronto plot where Roland had his dreams
Did sunlit shafts in the sylvan wood remind him of Gossamer beams?
Do you hear the echo of yesteryear as you pass Mud Corner by?
Did the boys now dust beneath your feet hear the winds wistful sigh?

As in a dream Roland picked the violets blue all down Regent Street
A carpet blue that filled his soul as he went forth to meet,
The fate that had been ordained for him on another field of blood
And at Plugstreet Wood for evermore the violets blue will bud!

Tony Spagnoly.

Roland Leighton's headstone at Louvencourt Military Cemetery, France.

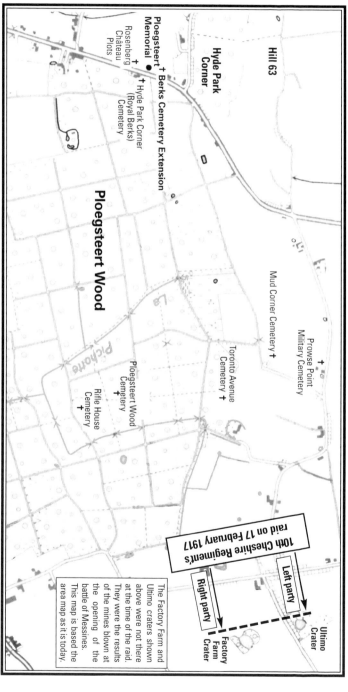

Hyde Park Corner

Hill 63

Ploegsteert † † Berks Cemetery Extension
Memorial ●

Rosenberg
Château
Plots

† Hyde Park Corner
(Royal Berks)
Cemetery

Ploegsteert Wood

Mud Corner Cemetery †

Prowse Point
Military Cemetery

Toronto Avenue
Cemetery †

Ploegsteert Wood
Cemetery †

Rifle House
Cemetery †

Pichamo

10th Cheshire Regiment's raid on 17 February 1917

Left party

Right party

Factory
Farm
Crater

Ultimo
Crater

The Factory Farm and
Ultimo craters shown
above were not there
at the time of the raid.
They were the results
of the mines blown at
the opening of the
battle of Messines.
This map is based the
area map as it is today.

MEEANEE DAY, a Battle Honour awarded to the Cheshire Regiment on 7 February 1843, holds particular significance to men of the Regiment's 10th Battalion. On that day in 1917 a 10th Battalion raid conducted against the German Factory Farm fortifications northeast of Ploegsteert Wood resulted in heavy casualties amongst the raiding party. The names of 33 of the fallen are commemorated on the Ploegsteert Memorial and 18 are buried in The Berks extension Cemetery at Hyde Park corner.

70

*I Salute the Glorious Dead who did not live
to see the Success of their Endeavour.*
Roger Keyes

7
CHESHIRES IN THE WOOD
10th, 11th and 13th Battalions, The Cheshire Regiment,
MEEANEE DAY, 17 February 1917.

VISITORS TO THE MILITARY CEMETERIES at Hyde Park Corner north of Ploegsteert will note the many headstones featuring the Cheshire Regiment's cap badge – 34 in the Berks Cemetery Extension and 14 in the Royal Berks (Hyde Park Corner) Cemetery just across the road. Panels 4 and 5 of the Ploegsteert Memorial itself lists a further 108 with no known graves, while 12 are buried in Rifle House Cemetery within Ploegsteert Wood, one in La Plus Douve Farm Cemetery and one in Ration Farm (La Plus Douve) Annexe another 8 are to be found in St. Quentin Cabaret Military Cemetery and, still in the Ploegsteert Sector, 8 lay at rest in London Rifle Brigade Cemetery, 34 in Tancrez Farm Cemetery and 3 in Nieppe Communal Cemetery.

Those who died of their wounds in Dressing Stations, Field Ambulances, and Casualty Clearing Stations in the area add to the tally: 6 in Pont-de-Nieppe; 4 in Pont-d'Achelles; one at Trois Arbres; 14 at Hazebrouck Communal Cemetery, 5 in th Bailleul Communal Cemetery [Nord] with another 88 in it's Extension.

The Ploegsteert Memorial.

Royal Berks (Hyde Park Corner) Cemetery.

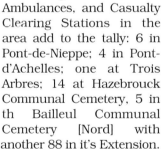

The Cheshire Regimental cap badge.

The Berks Cemetery Extension.

All pay tribute to the Regiment's sacrifice in this supposedly 'quiet' sector of the Western Front during the Great War of 1914-18.

Of the 108 Cheshire names listed on the Ploegsteert Memorial, 33 are those of men of the 10th Battalion who fell on 17 February 1917 whilst, in the Berks Cemetery Extension, 17 of the 18 men of that battalion also fell on 17 February, the 18th dying a day later, presumably of wounds incurred in the action of the day before, a day which holds particular significance to the Cheshire Regiment.

Known as MEEANEE DAY, 17 February is the date of a regimental Battle Honour celebrated in memory of that date in 1843, when General Sir Charles J. Napier's small force of 2,500 men made up of Indian infantry and cavalry and one British unit, The Cheshire Regiment, defeated 30,000 of the Baluchi Army of the Ameers of Scinde at Meeanee. An account of the battle by Major-General W. F. P. Napier (Sir Charles' brother) records:

> Such was the battle of Meeanee, fought on the 17th of February 1843, with two thousand men against more than thirty thousand. It was in its general arrangements, in all that depended on the commander, a model of skill and intrepidity combined; and in its details fell nothing short of any recorded deeds of arms. The front of battle was a chain of single combats, where no quarter was given, none called for, none expected; Sepoys and Europeans and Beloochs were alike bloody and remorseless, taking life for life, giving death for death. The ferocity on both sides was unbounded, the carnage horrible. The General, seeing a 22nd (Cheshire Regiment) soldier going to kill an exhausted Belooch chief, called to him to spare; the man drove his bayonet deep, and then turning, justified the act with a homely expression, terrible in its truthfulness accompanying such a deed: "This day, General, the shambles have it all to themselves."[1]

During the Great War 74 years later, 17 February 1917 saw three of the Cheshire Regiment's battalions serving on the Western Front in Southern Belgium – its 10th, 11th and 13th Battalions assigned to the 25th Division's 7th, 75th and 74th Brigades respectively.

On 31 October 1916, having moved north from the Somme, the 25th Division had set up its Headquarters at Bailleul in Northern France close to the Franco/Belgian border from where it took over the Ploegsteert Sector just across the frontier in Southern Belgium. Its line covered a front spanning 6,000 yards from the River Lys on its right, northward to Hill 63 at Ploegsteert (Hill 63 was later manned by the 36th [Ulster] Division when St. Yves was made the 25th's northern boundary). It was to serve in this sector until 24 February 1917 when it withdrew to St. Omer in Northern France.

On 21 March 1917 the Division, with The New Zealand Division and 3rd Australian Division, became part of II ANZAC CORPS, returning to the area to man the Wulverghem sector, the left of the II ANZAC CORPS line just west of Messines and north of Ploegsteert, to play its part in the opening of the Battle of Messines in June 1917.

11th Battalion, 75th Brigade

The 11th Battalion did not take part in a recorded action in early 1917 but on Christmas Day 1916 it was involved in a raid on German trenches in the Le Gheer road area southeast of Ploegsteert Wood.

Originally intended as a two-pronged attack on trenches north and south of the road, it was changed to target only the southern section when the Germans were found to be working on their wire north of the road. After a short, intensive bombardment starting at 8.30 pm, a raiding party of 3 Officers and 28 Other Ranks, after experiencing difficulty getting through German wire concealed in a ditch, successfully entered the enemy trenches at a point about 40 yards south of the road. Here they set up bombing blocks, killed four and captured one German and fired on a number of others running toward their trenches north of the road. The raiders returned to their lines after about 28 minutes with a prisoner, the identity of the German division facing them, and the knowledge that the enemy casualty rate was a deal higher than the four killed early in the raid due to accurate bombing and rifle fire and the supporting bombardment which, after its initial barrage on the targeted trenches, was maintained at a distance north and south of the point of entry.

Early in the New Year the battalion was relieved and withdrew to billets in Nieppe with the rest of the Brigade for a general clean-up and a strenuous training programme. Two weeks later they were back in the line relieving the 74th Brigade in the division's southern Le Touquet sector where they spent stints in and out of the line for the rest of January and well into February, alternating with support and rest periods in Le Bizet and Pont-de-Nieppe. These periods in the line involved repairing and generally improving the trenches while under frequent enemy bombardments and occasional raids, all in freezing cold conditions. A particularly heavy trench mortar box barrage on 15 February, two days before MEEANEE, enabled the enemy to enter a section of the Cheshire's trenches, capturing three men whose post was isolated by the barrage.

For MEEANEE, there was no recorded activity – the Battalion War Diary noting only the events of the days before and after:

Le Bizet: 16/2/17 – *The battalion was relieved by the 8th Border Regt. and moved into support at Le Bizet. As the thaw was now continuing rapidly the battalion was fully occupied with working parties in the trenches.*

18/2/17 – *Major the Hon. W. E. Guinness left the battalion to take up the appointment of Brigade Major to the 74th Brigade*

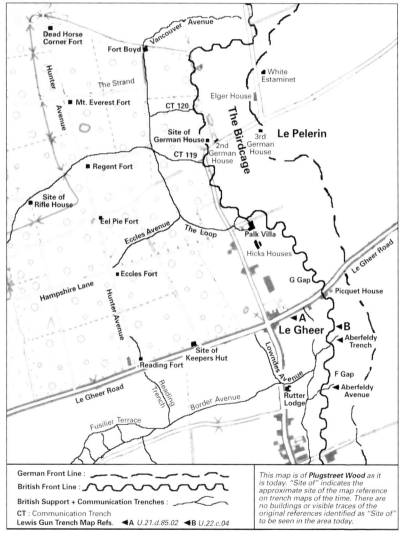

The 13th Battalion's positions during the German raid on 22 January 1917.

On 20 February the battalion, with the rest of 75th Brigade was withdrawn from the line and moved back to Nieppe and later onward to a training area in St. Omer with the rest of the 25th Division.[2]

13th Battalion, 74th Brigade*

The 13th Battalion was the next to see action, but it was a defensive one as, this time, it was the enemy who did the raiding.

Having spent periods in and out of the line inter-dispersed with patrolling, wiring, trench repairs, route-marching, kit inspections, training and lectures on Lewis guns, bombing and sniping the battalion found itself relieving the 9th Loyal North Lancs in the line on the morning of 22 January 1917.

With H.Q. set up at *Rifle House*, its companies were deployed as:– one in the line from *Vancouver Avenue* to *Communication Trench 120*; one from here to a machine gun post near *Palk Villa*; another continued the line to *G Gap* just north of the Le Gheer road, and a fourth from *G Gap* to *Aberfeldy Trench* south of the road.

A quiet morning was followed by a hectic afternoon when, at 1.40 pm, an enemy bombardment of shrapnel and explosive shells inter-dispersed with gas shells targeted the front, paying particular attention to *Lowndes Avenue, Hunter Avenue,*[3] and *Keepers Hut*. By 4.45 the situation at *Picquet House* on the Le Gheer Road south of *G Gap* was so bad that, expecting an attack, the support battalion was called up and, with all its fighting troops now in the line, its band, pioneers, police and servants, were moved up to reinforce the *Keepers Hut* breastworks.

As expected, the raid was launched when 75-150 of the enemy were seen leaving their trenches south of the Le Gheer road. Forming into two groups, one party was soon making its way north in the direction of *Picquet House* and the other southward to *F Gap*.

The move on *Piquet House* was effectively repulsed by Lewis gun fire

from a post sited at *28.U.21.d.85.02* before it reached the Cheshires' wire, but to the south the second party numbering 15-20 men, despite heavy Lewis gun and rifle fire, managed to penetrate *F Gap* and reached *Rutter Lodge* before making north for *Lowndes Avenue*. Here the raiders came under

Hunter Avenue in 1918.

*See map on Page 74 opposite for the map reference positions shown in italics.

accurate Lewis gun fire from a position at *28.U.22.c.04* causing them to veer towards *Aberfeldy Avenue* where, at the junction with the Cheshire's front line, their raid came to a sudden, abrupt and bloody end when one of their own minenwerfer shells dropped amongst them. Later, four German helmets were found amongst a mass of flesh and blood in the shattered section of the trench together with quantities of 'stick' bombs, explosives, shovels, Verey lights and their pistols.

One German seen leaving the Cheshire trench attempting to make his way back to his own lines was shot, wounded and brought back to the Cheshires lines for interrogation. He turned out to be the officer in charge of the raiding party.

In the meantime another German raid had penetrated trenches held by the 11th Lancashire Fusiliers holding the line left of the Cheshires front at the northern edge of Ploegsteert Wood. An S.O.S. rocket fired from *St. Yves Avenue* gave the alert of an attack when a Lancashire Fusiliers' officer reported that the Germans had broken into his positions and, from there, were bombing their way down to the Cheshires' left sector. Again, all available men were brought into the firing line, this time rushed up to the head of *Vancouver Avenue* to form a block and successfully cut off the advance.

The shelling, apart from a short period of intensity about 9 pm, eased by late evening and, during the night, working parties were sent

A Panoramic British 'trench-eye-view' of Le Gheer ....

out to clear-up and repair *Communication Trenches 119* and *120* and *Eccles Avenue* and *Lowndes Avenue,* the latter being found to be completely demolished.

The battalion was kept active with repairing wire, improving trenches and patrolling for the following four days. Much minenwerfer shelling was experienced (and effectively silenced with retaliatory trench mortar fire), and enemy aircraft kept the battalion's Lewis Gunners busy. On the morning of 26 January the battalion was relieved and withdrawn to the support lines only to be back in the front on the 30th, relieved again 3 days later and then moved with the 74th Brigade to Divisional Reserve in the Nieppe area across the border in Northern France. Reinforcements from England were absorbed into the battalion and intensive brigade, battalion and company attack training became the order of the day until 20 February when the Brigade made its way westwards to St. Omer for further instruction, training and reorganisation.

The battalion's war diary entry for MEEANEE DAY 1917 reads:

17.2.17. Sat: *The Battalion marched to the Brigade Training Ground and took part with the other Battalions of the Brigade in the attack*

Dinners on return to camp at 1.30 pm.

Afternoon. Half Holiday. Games etc.

2 pints of beer was issued to each man to celebrate Meeanee Day, the expense being borne by Regt. Funds.

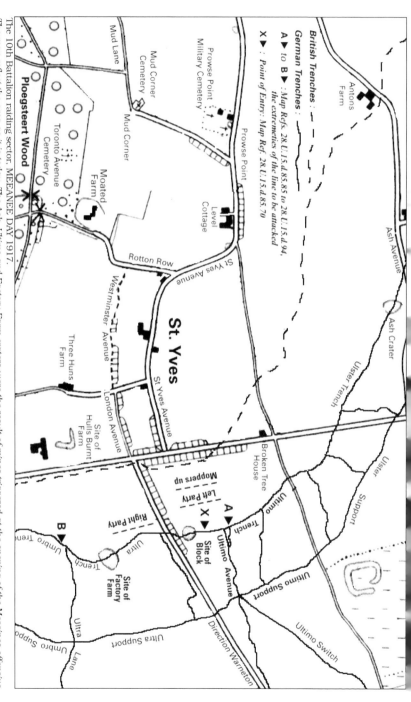

British Trenches :
German Trenches :

A ▼ to B ▼ : Map Refs. 28.U.15.d.85.85 to 28.U.15.d.94,
the extremeties of the line to be attacked
X ▼ : Point of Entry: Map Ref. 28.U.15.d.85.70

Antons Farm

Prowse Point Military Cemetery

Mud Lane

Mud Corner Cemetery

Mud Corner

Ploegsteert Wood

Toronto Avenue Cemetery

Moated Farm

Prowse Point

Level Cottage

Ash Avenue

Ash Crater

Rotton Row

St Yves Avenue

Westminster Avenue

Ulster Trench

St. Yves

St Yves Avenue

Three Huns Farm

London Avenue

Site of Hulls Burnt Farm

Ulster

Broken Tree House

Ulster Support

Moppers up

Left Party

Right Party

Ultra Trench

A ▼

X

Site of Block

Ultimo Avenue

Ultimo Trench

B ▼

Umbro Trench

Site of Factory Farm

Ultra Lane

Ultra Support

Umbro Support

Ultra Support

Umbro Support

Ultimo Support

Direction Warneton

Ultimo Switch

The 10th Battalion raiding sector. MEEANEE DAY 1917.
The map reflect the area as it is today. The Ash, Ultimo and Factory Farm craters were the result of mines triggered at the opening of the Messines offensive
in June 1917, 4 months after the Cheshire's raid.

78

So the 13th Battalion commemorated its MEEANEE DAY with a half day's holiday playing games and drinking two pints of beer per man.[4]

10th Battalion, 7th Brigade*

For the 10th Battalion, MEEANEE DAY was very well recorded, but was a day of mixed and contrasting emotions as the battalion was involved in a successful but casualty-costly raid on German positions north of *Factory Farm*, a well fortified German strongpoint below the southern shoulder of the Messines Ridge.

Following attack training on marked-out enemy trenches at Romarin, together with the systematic shelling of the actual German lines, the battalion's raiding party left Regina Camp and assembled in their take-off positions 20 minutes ahead of Zero. They were to launch a three-wave attack on enemy's trenches between reference points *28.U.15.d.94* & *28.U.15.d.85.85*, the first wave [right party] attacking between Factory Farm itself and the road north of it, the second wave [left party] north of the same road and the third wave [moppers up] following the second wave through the enemy wire.

At 10.40 am, under a hurricane barrage, the attack launched, but most of the shelling had missed the front line, falling behind the enemy fortifications and, half way across No-Man's Land, the first wave came under heavy, but inaccurate, machine gun fire from *Factory Farm*, fortunately causing only a few casualties. Leading the party, a Private J Kennedy, no less than 70 yards ahead of the right party, signalled to those following to bear left when he found there were no gaps in the German wire. On doing so they found the wire was badly damaged but also impossible to get through. The raiders then came under fire from a machine gun nest in the German front line about 50 yards north of *Factory Farm* which was effectively silenced when Lance Corporal Gerald, standing in the German wire, shouldered his Lewis Gun and emptied a complete drum into the position. With a second machine gun opening fire from their left the Cheshires responded with Lewis Guns, rifles and bombs hoping their second wave left party would break through the German front and ease the situation. They took cover in shell holes under intensive enemy bombing, machine gun and rifle fire and, after a short while, with no support coming from their left and with little chance of breaching the wire, orders were issued for them to withdraw, during which time they were to suffer casualties from both enemy machine gun and shellfire.

The left party on reaching the German wire found a gap about *U.15.d.85.70* and, although under heavy fire from just south of the double headed *Ultimo Avenue* communication trench, Lance-Corporal

See map on Page 78 opposite for map references shown in italics.

Ultimo Crater the site of the block which stopped the Cheshire bombers link to the right raiding party.

The road and distant site of Factory Farm (now a crater) seen from the German block position.

Upturned concrete structure found in the crater where once stood Factory Farm after the mines were triggered at the opening of the Battle of Messines.

L/Cpl. Nichols.

G. H Nichols knocked-out the machine gun team with his Lewis Gun just before a shell from the Cheshires' covering artillery fire scored a direct hit on the gun nest, destroying it. The raiders entered the German *Ultimo Trench* and a squad detached to form a wire block about 30 yards beyond the head of *Ultimo Avenue*.

A group of about 20 Germans outside of their dugouts were immediately attacked and killed, while another group seen running back to its support lines were shot on the run. Separate bombing parties quickly made their way north and south along the trench causing mayhem in the eight dugouts and one large concrete shelter in the trench section. There were about four Germans in each of the dugouts and about a dozen in the shelter. All of them refused to come out and were bombed where they stood. The bombing party working south to link with the first wave party were unable to reach and cross the road where the enemy had sited a strongly manned block guarding both the road and the trench leading to *Factory Farm,* which the first party had failed to penetrate. They made their way back, contributing to the carnage in and around the dugouts, a carnage helped along by their R.E. party blowing up a bomb dump 30 yards south of the head of *Ultimo Avenue.* The job done, and with no casualties suffered, the raiders, withdrew at approximately 11.10 am. Unfortunately the withdrawal was costly as a German sniper had marked down the ladders which had been put up to help the withdrawal and this, together with machine fire sweeping No-Man's Land took a heavy toll of them.

In the meantime the third party moppers-up suffered casualties from machine gun fire before reaching and crossing the German front trench. They split into two squads, one making its way along the top of the northern stretch of *Ultimo Avenue* which was empty of the enemy, closely followed by the second squad in the southern section.

Reaching the *Ultimo Support* trench they attacked the occupants with bombs, killing many and causing general havoc in the trench section. Some of the men made their way north along the support trench killing a considerable number of Germans by bombing them in their already shell-damaged dugouts. However this squad was unable to hold its own against superior numbers of the enemy that appeared and, owing to casualties, was forced to withdraw, unable to bring back 6 or 7 of their dead. Only eight men, three of them wounded were able to get away. The rest of the party in the support line accounted for a number of the enemy before being overrun – only one of this party were able to make it back. The rest of the moppers up had come under sniper and machine gun fire from right and rear and were unable to move forward to help those in the support line. In the meantime they had taken 10 prisoners near a dugout at the junction of *Ultimo Avenue* but eight of these were killed by their own machine gun fire on the way back across No-Man's Land with the withdrawing Cheshires.

The Battalion Diary for the day reads:

February 17th. MEEANEE DAY. *At 10.40 AM. One officer and 65 other ranks from A. C & D Coys under CAPT. I. S. APPLETON successfully raided the enemy's trenches north of FACTORY FARM between points U.15.d.94 & U.15.d.85.85 inflicting heavy casualtiess upon the enemy – Many dugouts were bombed. Bomb dumps & trench material destroyed. Ten prisoners were taken however 8 of this number were caught by their own M/G fire & killed crossing NO MAN'S LAND to our line. Officer's leading parties were:–*

CAPT. I. S. APPLETON (in command) 2nd LIEUT ROWE (A Coy) 2nd LIEUT NICHOLLS (C Coy) 2nd LIEUT MANNING (D Coy).

2nd LIEUT MANNING died of wounds. 2nd LIEUT NICHOLLS & 2nd LIEUT BLES [sic] (presumably ROWE) wounded.

February 18th. *Situation normal Relieved by 3rd WORCESTERSHIRE REGT in accordance with BATT ORDER No.171*

Patrols were sent out into N.Ms.L. to search for wounded & dead & were successful in recovering 15 wounded & dead.

After its relief by the 3rd Worcesters, the battalion marched to Regina Camp back at Romarin and, starting on the 19th, spent a few days of cleaning-up, re-fitting and general brigade training before the 7th Brigade was replaced by the 1st New Zealand Rifle Brigade and moved to new billets at Nieppe and thereafter to St Omer with the rest of the 25th Division.

Total casualties for the 10th Battalion were recorded in an action report written on the following day [18 Feb.] were noted as:

Officers	– wounded	3	(1 since died of wounds)
O.R.	– killed	28	
	wounded	63	
	missing	27	

The report also noted that a number of the wounded were known to have got back to the Aid Post without giving their names and that efforts were being made to trace them to enable updating of the records.[5]

So ended MEEANEE DAY for the three Cheshire battalions at Ploegsteert in 1917: the 10th counting the costs of a raid on the German front line; the 11th in freezing cold support lines at Le Bizet repairing trenches, and the 13th at rest in Divisional Reserve at Nieppe enjoying a half day holiday and 2 pints of beer per man.

Notes:

1. In his work *The Conquest of Scinde* written in 1844, Major-General W.F.P. Napier describes the battle of Meeanee in graphic terms. The 'General' that the author refers to is his brother, General Sir Charles James Napier, G.C.B. Miani (Anglicised as Meeanee) is now in Pakistan}.

2. Casualties for the raid were one killed and six slightly wounded. The body of the soldier who died, Private William Bishop, was never recovered and his name is commemorated on the Ploegsteert Memorial.

3. Hunter Avenue was [and still is] a ride traversing Ploegsteert Wood from the Le Gheer road directly northward to the wartime-named Dead Horse Corner at the junction with Rotten Row which itself leads into St. Yves Avenue forming the corner where Bruce Bairnsfather's cottage stood. 6 concrete fort/pillboxes were [and still are] sited along its length. It was used as a breastworked support 'trench' in the war [see map on page 74].

St Yves Avenue was named after the small hamlet that was sited on the north east area of the wood. The hamlet was razed to the ground in the 1914 fighting and was never rebuilt after the war, Another hamlet, St. Yvon was established on the north western edge of the wood after the war..

4. Of the 13th Battalion's 17 burials in the Berks Cemetery Extension, seven lost their lives in the action of 22 January.

5. In Arthur Crookenden's *History of the Cheshire Regiment During the Great War 1914-1918* the casualty listing of the raid given as 40 killed and 60 wounded.

The final count of the 10th Battalion's dead is 54. Of this number 35 are commemorated on the Ploegsteert Memorial as having no known graves. Of its 18 casualties buried in the Berks Cemetery Extension, 17 died the day of the raid. A further two died of their wounds at Bailleul aid stations and are buried in the Bailleul Communal Cemetery Extension [Nord].

Of the 17 Cheshires in the Berks Extension Cemetery who died on 17 February, one headstone is of an unknown soldier. On the Ploegsteert Memorial is listed Lance-Corporal 53055 Peter Capper who died in the raid. A letter to his mother dated 13 March 1917 from a fellow Lance-Corporal and close friend Herbert Holt who was in the same raiding party describes how Peter Capper fell, mentioning that "he was buried in a little cemetery at Hyde Park Corner". It is believed that the unknown Cheshire soldier in the Berks Extension Cemetery is in fact Lance-Corporal Capper. Efforts are currently in process to arrange for a new headstone bearing his name to replace the existing headstone.

St Yves Avenue Communication Trench with No-Man's Land on the horizon.

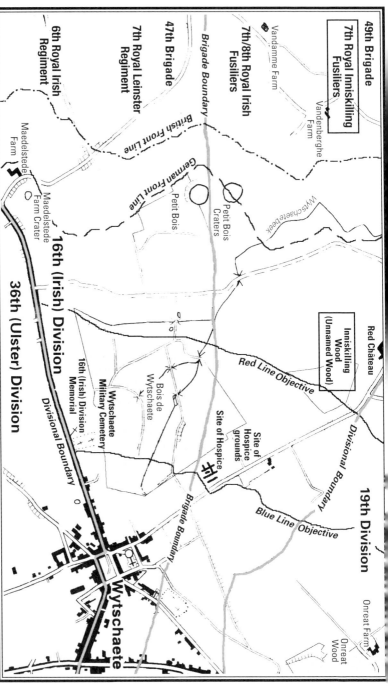

Unnamed Wood, renamed Inniskilling Wood by Divisional Commander, Maj.-Gen. W. B. Hickie showing his appreciation of the 7th Inniskillings in the 49th Brigade' attack on the opening day of the Battle of Messines. (*Detail overprinted on an adaptation of today's map of the area*).

The deeds of Erin's brave will endure ...
as long as Martial tales are told.
Anon.

8
THE NAMING OF UNNAMED WOOD
7th Battalion Royal Inniskilling Fusiliers
The Battle of Messines, Wytschaete, 7 June 1917

THE BATTLE OF MESSINES in June 1917 was an excellent example of planning, development and execution making the best use of all available arms, resulting in the first totally successful British operation since the outbreak of the war.

Whereas enemy defenders along the Messines Ridge were aware that an attack was due, confirmed by British aircraft sorties, constant troop movement, general attack preparation and days of intensive bombardment, they had no idea of the devastating surprise the opening of the assault would bring. 19 deep-tunnelled mines, using some 500 tons of ammonal, driven-in below German strongpoints along the western slopes of the ridge were triggered at 3.10 am on 7 June, their explosions being the signal launching waves of infantry attacks along its length from Mount Sorrel to St Yves. Everything else went to plan – almost to the minute. The British infantry quickly overran everything in its path, taking its first line objectives on schedule, then pausing to let the second wave battalions leap-frog through to their targets until all the objectives of the first phase of the attack were successfully met. Then the second phase divisions took over the job and the days fighting ended with an incredibly successful attack, incurring well below the estimated casualty-count for all battalions involved.

The road running from Kemmel to Wytschaete, map-referenced as *Suicide Road*, had seen much action during the Great War, but nothing like what it was to experience that morning. The stretch of it running from Maedelstede Farm to Wytschaete and on along the road through the village, formed the Divisional Boundary between the 16th (Irish) Division and the 36th (Ulster) Division – the first time these Irish divisions would go into action alongside each other, a unique gathering of Irishmen, over 30,000 of them.

The Royal Inniskilling Fusiliers had five of its battalions serving amongst both divisions: the 7th and 8th with 49th Brigade of the former, and the 9th, 10th and 11th with 109th Brigade of the latter.[1]

British pilot's-eye-view over the ground covered by the 16th (Irish) Division.

Unnamed Wood

Hospice

Bois de Wytschaete

Wytschaete

Petit Bois

German Front Line

86

When the Petit Bois and Maedelstede Farm mines blew in the 16th Division's sector, the 7th Inniskillings and 7/8th Irish Fusiliers led the 49th Brigade's attack with the 8th Inniskillings following as 'moppers up'.[2] Their objectives, designated as *Red Line* and *Blue Line* were reached and overran in good time but, as expected, vicious fighting was experienced before reaching the *Blue Line*. Capturing the heavily fortified *Unnamed Wood* and *Hospice Redoubt* on the road running north of Wytschaete, took its toll. The local Hospice and its grounds had been transformed into a formidable strongpoint by the Germans and, standing on this high point it commanded an all important view of the valley below. Equally as intimidating was the wood alongside it map-referenced as *Unnamed Wood* by army cartographers of the period, but the *Hospice Redoubt* saw the heaviest fighting of the day for the Irishmen. It took three-and-a-half hours of bitter fighting before the German garrison conceded defeat.

The battalions set about consolidating the line which they completed by 6.50 am. The 2nd Royal Irish Regiment then leap-frogged through to continue the attack on the *Green Line* and *Black Line* objectives atop the ridge itself. Wytschaete village, a veritable fortress surrounded by trenches and carefully sited machine gun nesst in its cellars and buildings was expected to be a major problem for the attacking troops. They were pleasantly surprised to find that heavy bombardment days before the opening of the battle had left it no more than a pile of crumbling ruins. In the meantime battalions of the 36th (Ulster) Division in action south of the divisional boundary had been equally as successful in meeting its objectives. What was left of the Wytschaete village square then saw Irish troops of both divisions, men from Ireland's North and South, sharing together a celebration of achievement.

It was evident that the 49th Brigade had scored a major success in taking these two strongpoints and, on 11 June, four days after the opening of the battle, Divisional Commander, Maj.-Gen. W. B. Hickie showed his appreciation of the part played by the 7th Inniskillings at *Unnamed Wood* by renaming it *Inniskilling Wood*, and had a sign erected accordingly.[4] Now privately owned woodland, it has signs forbidding entry to its rides and pathways, but on that June morning in 1917, nothing was able to forbid men of the 7th Inniskillings entry to them. North of the wood from the *Hospice Redoubt* stood *Red Château* where today stands a cottage, its position edging what was then a sunken road, the remains of its original course still visible alongside the more embanked road of today. *Red Château* did cause problems to the advancing Irishmen and it was the sunken road that

The 16th (Irish) Division'sbird's-eye-view of the Hospice Redoubt position. The Hospice and its grounds were never rebuilt after the destruction of 1917, its site now housing a football pitch.

The football pitch in the old Hospice grounds with Inniskilling Wood edging it.

The rebuilt 'Red Château' today, with Inniskilling Wood in the right background.

sheltered them from machine gun fired from the Hollandscheschuur strongpoint but, like all obstacles on that day, it soon fell to them.

At the outset of the attack, the 6th Royal Irish Regiment of 47th Brigade, to the right of the Inniskillings and Irish Fusiliers moved forward accompanied by 56-year old Major William Hoey Kearney Redmond, an Irish Nationalist MP. On his return from Ireland after a bout of illness, had been posted to the divisional staff and had pleaded with his superiors to be allowed to join the attack with his old battalion. This they agreed to, but on the condition that he went only as far as the first objective. As soon as the battalion advanced, he was hit in the leg and then the hand. Stretcher-bearers of the 36th (Ulster) Division initially carried him to their dressing station for treatment and then on to the 16th Field Ambulance near Paraines Farm on *Suicide Road* where shock set in and he died. His body was laid out in the chapel of the Convent of St. Antoine at Locre which housed the divisional staff and, on the evening of 8 June, he was buried in the convent garden alongside a grotto to the Virgin Mary.

For many years after the war his grave was tended by the nuns, but later, at the request of his family, his remains were exhumed and reburied outside the walls of the British military plot across

Maj. William Redmond.

Nuns of the Convent of St. Antoine with village children laying flowers at Major William Redmond's grave alongside a grotto to the Virgin Mary in the convent garden.

the road from the convent, today's Locre Hospice Cemetery, He had made it quite clear that, should he be killed, on no condition would he be buried in a British cemetery and, although the Commonwealth War Graves Commission have offered to rebury him in the military cemetery on a number of occasions, his family have faithfully honoured his wishes, refusing to move him to within its walls.[3]

In the post war years the local community erected a Memorial in the form of a Celtic Cross to the 16th (Irish) Division as a tribute to the men who liberated them from their German occupiers.

Consecrated in 1926 by Divisional Commander Hickie, it sits on a plot alongside the Wytschaete British Military Cemetery south of the village square on the road to Kemmel, or *Suicide Road* as it was known during the war – the old Divisional Boundary.

The 16th (Irish) Division's memorial alongside Wytschaete British Military Cemetery.

Further down the road on its way to Kemmel, on each side of the road respectively, at the approximate point on the boundary from which their attacks were launched are memorials to both the 16th (Irish) and 36th (Ulster) Divisions.

In November 1988 an Irish memorial was inaugerated commemorating both the 16th (Irish) and 36th (Ulster) together with the 10th Division.[5] It stands on the right hand side of the road, running southward out of Messines, but nowhere near where men of the 16th and 36th divisions fought and died alongside each other.

The Irish Divisional memorials either side of the boundary road from Wytschaete to Kemmel.

The New Zealand Division, part of Anzac II Corps, captured this part of the ridge during the battle in June 1917, the Irish divisions never having served in this sector during the Battle of

The Island of Ireland Memorial on the Messines–Ploegsteert road.

Messines. Word has it that the memorial, a symbol of appeasement, is so placed because Messines is where the Flemish community in this part of Belgium meets with the Walloon community to its south.

Nevertheless the memorial is a worthy tribute to all of those men from the Emerald Isle that served and fell in the Great War.[6]

Notes:

1. Later, in the Passchendaele battles of August 1917, these two Irish divisions were to fight alongside each other again, this time on the Frezenberg Ridge near Zonnebeke. but this time with tragic results. Rain, mud and a desperate German defence trapped the units from both divisions in the shell-shattered, waterlogged battlefield and serious losses were inflicted on them.

2. The two craters at Petit Bois are in open pastureland and are now full of water. A boring-machine, constructed from one used to tunnel the London Underground, was shipped to Belgium to assist in digging the tunnels for these craters. It was abandoned after consistently clogging in the Flemish mud and now lies 80 feet down toward the craters, still waiting to be rescued. The workings of the Petit Bois mine tunnels started at Vandamme Farm which is still on its original site.

3. Major Redmond believed that if Irishmen, regardless of religion or political beliefs, could fight and die together, they could surely live together. The Convent of St. Antoine was badly damaged during the 1918 battles and was rebuilt a 100 metres or so away from its original site.

4. 2nd-Lieut. T. J. Dalton (4th Royal Irish Regiment attd. 7th inniskillings) died of wounds on 9 June 1917. He is buried at Etaples Military Cemetery near Boulogne. Plot XVII, Row A, Grave 21. The battalion loss at the wood was 14 dead, 127 wounded [5 later died of wounds] and missing.

5. The 10th Division never saw action on the Western Front but was to suffer losses of over 9.000 men during its service in Gallipoli, Greece, Egypt, Palestine and the Lebanon.

6. On 11 November 1998, the 80th anniversary of the Armistice, *The Island of Ireland Peace Park* was opened by the President of Ireland in the company of HRH Queen Elizabeth II and HM King Albert of Belgium. It aims to promote peace in Ireland by commemorating the Irish men and women who died in the Great War.

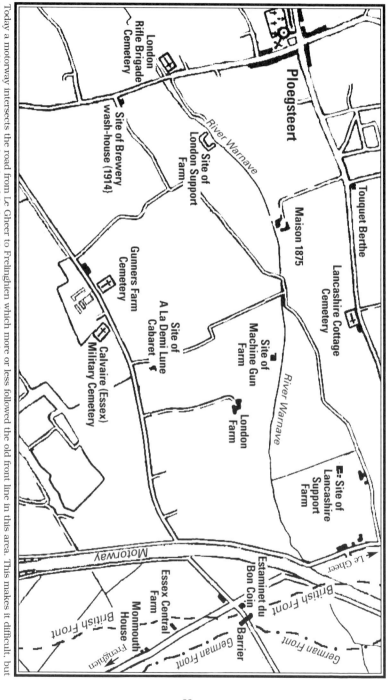

Today a motorway intersects the road from Le Gheer to Frelinghien which more or less followed the old front line in this area. This makes it difficult, but not impossible, to access certain lengths of the line without a major diversion by car or coach. Walking is not recommended.

War is a delight for those with no experience of it.
Erasmus.

9
THE L.R.B. AT PLUGSTREET

5th (City of London) Regiment (The London Rifle Brigade)
Ploegsteert, November 1914 – April 1915

THE VOLUNTEER MOVEMENT had always played its part in Britain's military history being of vital importance to the country's defence in the early days of the French Revolution as well as in 1804 when the French were preparing to cross the Channel. The weaknesses in the Regular Army shown in the 1854-1856 Crimean War eventually caused the movement to become an integral part of the country's military organisation when, in May 1859, the Secretary of State for War authorised the Lord-Lieutenants of Counties throughout the land to raise their own Volunteer Corps. In a short time units had been formed all over the country, with thousands of men being kitted out and commencing regular training. In keeping with this, the Lord Mayor of London put forward a proposition that the City raise a volunteer unit, resulting in the formation of the 1st London Volunteer Rifle Corps (City of London Volunteer Brigade).[1]

Created to meet periods of danger, volunteer units tended to be forgotten or disbanded when the threat had passed. Such periods were rare and, in the intervening years, the volunteers were seen as something of a joke, not taken seriously and left to determine their own means of survival. These attitudes were partly overcome when Lord Haldine, in his 1908 Army Reform, created the Territorial Force, a citizen army with organisation and training similar to that of the regulars. The existing London units were reorganised into Territorial Battalions of The London Regiment, each affiliated to a Regular Army battalion. With the London Rifle Volunteer Corps, now the 5th (City of London) Regiment (London Rifle Brigade) better known as the London Rifle Brigade or L.R.B., the affiliation was with The Rifle Brigade.[2]

Being a member of the L.R.B, as with others of the London territorial units, was slightly elitist, seen more as belonging to a private social club, the sporting events and social activities being as much an attraction to members as its military *raison d'être*. Its muster was made up primarily from London's middle classes – city office workers, school teachers, bank employees and the like who, as volunteers, were expected to cover their own expenses, buy their own uniforms and accoutrements – and pay a membership fee. With Haldene's Territorial Regiments came the khaki uniform, supplied to the men free, as were accoutrements and weaponry, but it was mid-1916 before the L.R.B. had its membership fee cancelled.

Standards of training and discipline in the territorials were generally high and, with the L.R.B., the standard of musketry was exceptional. Nevertheless, the opinion of many professional soldiers of the time was that 'citizen soldier' battalions, well suited for Home Service, could never be used in battle against a professional army.

This prejudice changed in 1914 when the first Territorial Units left for France to give much needed support to the battle-depleted regulars. Following its retreat from Mons, the battles of the Marne, the Aisne and the coming of First Ypres, the B.E.F. was defending by the skin of its teeth a dangerously thin line in the mud of Flanders and Northern France. This line was not the sophisticated system of front, support, reserve and communication trenches integrated with well-placed and fortified strongpoints that were the norm from 1915 onwards. The belligerents had been fighting a war of movement until October 1914 and were now entrenched in a line that was unstable to say the least. Parapets were washed away by rain, trench sides were constantly collapsing, the trenches were often waist-deep in water, communication trenches were little more than shallow ditches, the system of caring for and moving the wounded was in its infancy, and fever, sickness and 'trench feet' were taking their toll on the battalions in the line, causing casualties almost equal to those imposed on them by the opposing armies. Steel helmets, hand-grenades, trench mortars and a fighting airforce would not make their appearance until the following year and all types of materials – food, clothing, ammunition, guns and shells etc – were in painfully short supply. All in all, the Regular Army was in desperate need of re-enforcement – and this is where the Territorials were to prove themselves, dispelling all doubts about their ability to fight alongside Britain's regular regiments.

Mobilised at the beginning of August 1914, the L.R.B was one of the first territorials units to move to France. On 15 August, the War Office called on the Territorials to volunteer for service overseas, requiring a 75% agreement from a battalion. Lord Cairns commanding the L.R.B. immediately made claim to that figure. making the battalion, now part of 2nd London Brigade, 1st London Division. the first in the brigade to do so.[3] On 4 November it sailed for France as an attachment to the 11th Brigade, 4th Division then in the line on the Franco/Belgian border. Arriving at Le Havre on the 5th, it stayed overnight at a tented camp, with many of its troops sleeping in the open during a cold and frosty night. Next morning it entrained to St. Omer then, on the 8th, it moved to Wisques to billet in the Benedictine Convent which, with an extension being built, was empty, without water, light or heating facilities, but large enough to house the whole battalion. Here the men were faced with a discipline and training different to anything they had so far experienced.[4] Digging trenches, firing practice (with new rifles issued just before they left England) and attack-training were the order of a very long 8 days of preparing for the front. Coupled with the other Territorials in France, they were the only troops in reserve able to offer the back-up now so desperately needed by the B.E.F. following the close-down of First Ypres.

The battalion's mettle was tested on 16 November when, leaving Wisques, it marched in pouring rain the 17-miles to Hazebrouck on the notorious French *pavé* roads. This was followed on the 17th with a further 11-mile march on similar roads to Ballieul where it rested for two-days. Then it moved, in a blizzard, to Romarin in Belgium, where it billeted in the attics of civilian-inhabited houses. The weather throughout the month had seen torrential rain swamping the trench lines. Added to this on the 18th a hard frost set in which did a little to keep down the mud, On the 19th, the L.R.B. was officially attached to the 4th Division's 11th Brigade. The next day, half-companies went into the trenches in Ploegsteert Wood, starting their new life with the regulars.[5] The remaining half-companies did the same in the days following and, on one of these 'tours', the battalion took its first casualty, a shell killing 18-year old Rifleman Jack L. Dunnett.[6] **

The battalion moved to billets in the village of Ploegsteert on the 22nd with its HQ in *Report Centre*, a farmhouse on the Ploegsteert-Messines road about 800 yards north of the village. Later the HQ moved to cottages east of the road closer to the billets. From then on, when not training, its time was taken up with fatigues earning it nicknames such as "The London Fatigue" and "The Fatigue Fifth".

From the 24th it alternated its time in the line with supplying work parties converting a ride in the wood (*Bunter Avenue)* into a reserve line.[7] It was also involved in the laying of paths through the wood itself

A serving rifleman during this period notes in his diary:

19 November: Snowing hard ... Marched into a village called Ploegsteert (Anglicised Plugstreet). Billeted in barns, lofts, and cottages ... Am now having coffee and chipped potatoes in an Estaminet, "pommes de terre frites," angliced into "Bombardier Fritz" by the Tommies.

20 November: Glorious morning, clear, bright and frosty. Snow everywhere ... Our platoon start for the firing line at 3.30 pm. ... Grand clear sunset over the snow ... We reached the reserve trenches and turned into barns for an hour ... Then, it being dark, we started along the road for the

**See Appendix B, page 107.

Track-laying in Ploegsteert Wood, 1914.

advanced trenches ... Here we were under fire for the first time; German snipers a few hundred yards away put some bullets over our heads.

21 November: ... bullets going 'smack' over our heads ... Germans 300 yards away ... We are with the Hampshires, learning the ropes so to speak ... We work in pairs at night in shifts ... Half the night I was in charge of a little party engaged in digging a communication trench to the rear. The clay is very stiff and frozen ... We have to fill our water-bottles at a ruined farm at night (*Essex Farm*), when the snipers cannot see us, and we have to make that do for the whole day.[8]

22 November: Last night we floundered out through an ice-bound communication trench to the reserve line in the wood. Water in our water-bottles frozen ... A great Crucifix stands amid the ruins of a hamlet (Le Gheer), the only thing undamaged. Incongruous with bullets whistling around ...

24 November: Back to H.Q.– barns; a filthy billet.

26 November: More landscape gardening in the wood.

28 November: Rain made the parapet slide into the trench – repairs all morning instead of sleep.

30 November: Left trenches last night and reached the barn at midnight – a terrible journey – worst experience I ever had. The mud and our fatigue combined made it a nightmare.

1 December: To-day we had a *hot bath* in a small brewery in Ploegsteert.

On 1 December, prior to sanitary arrangements being made official, the battalion made use of a brewery on the Ploegsteert–Armentières road as a wash-house, the large boilers being re-activated and its vats

The Brewery 'wash-house' in 1914.

The Brewery 'wash-house' site today.

used as wash tubs for the troops. This was the only time it was used for this purpose because the owner objected, causing it to be re-instated a 'disused' brewery. It was razed to the ground later in the war (by enemy bombardment, not by the L.R.B.). Although it was never rebuilt as a brewery, the buildings on its site today bear a striking resemblance to the brewery of old.

While the diarist and his platoon mates were enjoying their illegal bath on 1 December, British artillery set about bombarding *Factory Farm*, a German redoubt east of the wood, giving those of the battalion's troops in the wood a taste of a prolonged, but not hostile, bombardment together with the experience of being under shellfire (literally) as the British guns on Hill 63, fired across the wood to reach their target.

Later, they too received a much needed break when arrangements were made for a clean up a delousing and an overdue replacement of underclothes – the first bath the men had had since leaving England – in a brewery at Armentières (this one an official acquisition).

The rifleman's diary continues:

2 December: Navvying, making new trenches.

3 December: We have been issued with goat-skin coats – we look like Polar Explorers.

8 December: Back to the front line, we are taking over a stretch of our own.

12 December: I am in an Estaminet with 24 others, very comfortable ...

14 December: Still very comfortable at the Estaminet '*à St. Matthias*.' This afternoon, Blunden, Warwick and I procured a tub and some hot water, took it up to the loft, and had a hot bath. Just while we were drying the Germans shelled the village, uncomfortable position.

15 December: Digging reserve trenches – Bunhill Row – in the woods.

19 December: Left early in the morning to man reserve trenches in Bunhill Row. They are damp and sticky ... Our guns were keeping up a tremendous cannonade and soon the machine guns and rifles in front began. After some hours we were ordered out and marched up to a point close behind the front line.

With the 19 December attack on the *Birdcage*, the L.R.B. saw its first action, with two companies in support in *Bunhill Row* and two in reserve. Expecting a counter-attack after the attack, the support companies moved in pitch-darkness and heavy rain to the *Hunter Avenue* trench, a breastwork-lined ride traversing the wood from south to north.[9] Two half-companies spent the night consolidating the new line, the others spent it in the wood's marshy undergrowth.[10]

Following the action against the *Birdcage* the diary notes:

22 December: Marched to Armentières to a brewery on the banks of the Lys by the Pont de Nieppe to have hot baths ... we are all snowed under with parcels.

23 December: We are going up the line tonight.

On 23 December the company was attached to a regular battalions – all being in the line at the same time. On Christmas Eve the regulars went into rest in farms and billets behind the line, leaving the L.R.B. in the front. The battalion could now make claim to being the only territorial battalion to have held the whole of a regular brigade front (except for a half company on the extreme left of the line).

Meanwhile, the Saxon trenches opposite were seen to be lined with fairy lights with a number of Christmas trees in evidence, a precursor to the unique Christmas Truce of that year.

The rifleman's diary recorded the following:

Christmas Day: The paths (within the wood) are neatly labelled with names reminiscent of home, '*Piccadilly Circus*' etc ... last night was a cheerful one in the trenches and barricades. Everyone made merry with carols, mouth organs, and popular songs. The Germans also made a rare noise, and all along the line there was far more cheering and singing than shooting. To-day a number of our fellows and the Germans have been chatting between the lines, swopping cigarettes and so on.

L.R.B. and Saxon troops during the Christmas Truce.

26 December: ... some of the British are out talking to the Germans in the interval between our trenches ... Yesterday there were hundreds and hundreds of both sides, officers and men in between. We carried over some German dead to their lines and helped bury them. Their officer read some prayers,

98

and thanked (in English) 'his English friends' for bringing them over.

28 December: At present I am in what is left of a house. Except for a few beams {many broken) nothing is left of the roof. A guard lives in the cellar, while another man and I are snipers upstairs, but owing to the truce there is nothing to do. we can all see fraternising going on.

British and German troops mingled freely through the following week, but this all came to an end when a 'message from above' stated that automatic rifle fire would 'restart' the war on New Year's Day.[11]

On 4 January 1915 the battalion moved to new billets in Ploegsteert village preparing to taking over its own section of the line. While in billets the rifleman continued his account:

6 January: Back in billets ... cottage in Ploegsteert. At the Estaminet to-day there were 4 Jocks (Gordons) sitting round a table, all a little drunk, and solemnly singing some slow and plaintive air.

The day he was listening to his 'singing Jocks', his battalion moved into its new sector (*Essex Trench*) running from the River Warnave to the *Estaminet du Bon Coin* on the road to Le Touquet.[12]

In early January a redistribution of troops resulted in a reduction in brigade frontage and battalion sectors were narrowed to permit a single company being in the line with a second in support, while the two remaining companies rested in 'dry' billets.

The rifleman keeping is diary, obviously in 'dry' billets, continued with his story:

8 January: ... We walked up to the Crucifix at Le Gheer to collect some odds and ends of German equipment ... We got up unseen in a slight mist and secured some souvenirs.

10 January: Company Church Parade in a school-room (we are in billets).

14 January: Billeted this time in a factory in Armentières. Another hot bath in the brewery. About 12 of us sitting round in a vat, up to our necks and half hidden in steam, singing 'Drake goes West' at the top of our voices.

The L.R.B. saw its sector shortened to a position from 280 yards south of the Warnave to the estaminet, its front trench running parallel to the Le Gheer–Le Touquet road but about 50 yards in front of it. It worked its smaller frontage on a three-day turn around system, one company in the front line; its Support Company in a farm 300 yards southeast of the 'disused' brewery with the better part of one of its platoons in *London Farm*, a detachment in *Mountain Gun Farm*, and another in *Red House*. The Reserve Company went into billets in Ploegsteert as part of an 11th Brigade composite battalion, while the fourth rested and cleaned-up in Armentières. This way each company was able to served in the line for no more than a period of nine days before taking a rest period.

Meanwhile the rifleman, now seemingly a member of the brigade's composite battalion in Ploegsteert, was faithfully updating his diary and losing no time in enjoying his off-duty periods in reserve:

1 February: ... Have been sketching in the wood ...

2 February: Concert in Plugstreet. One of ours, Babington, is a baritone soloist at St. Peters, Eaton Square. He sang tonight – great success – jolly good concert. We had the piper too.

He eventually took his turn in the line in early February when:

6 February: ... made some panorama sketches of the enemy front line through periscopes.

11 February: At *Mountain Gun Farm.* The Guard Room is a little brick hut about 8 feet square. There is a log fire burning in the open hearth, a sentry stands outside the window, and the two others are sleeping beside me on the straw.

13 February: It is impossible to live through a dreary winter in this God-forsaken country without feeling very sorry for the unfortunate inhabitants. It is sad to see the smashed and blackened ruins of what was a prosperous neat little farm, and to think of what has happened to the hardworking peasant folk. Some of the farms we occupy in support line are within a few hundred yards of the front line, and in many cases the people still cling desperately to what is left. There are civilian people still at Mountain Gun Farm ...

Once the battalion became used to the system of manning its front, life was reasonably orderly. Shelling was intermittent and blowing mines did not take place in this area due to ground conditions. The main problems were avoiding sniper fire and coming to terms with living in, and moving through, cloying mud. The latter particularly affected the carrying parties who had to work during the night. The narrow lane leading to the trenches from the Ploegsteert–Armentières road was more like a ford, always awash with water and slime. On this road, within a few hundred yards of the trenches, a small inn, *A la Demi Lune Cabaret* in a field opposite *Essex House*, was used as a *materiels* dump with the owner earning a good living by selling coffee and beer to the troops (he was later shot as a spy when a telephone line was discovered running from his premises to the German lines).

The tracks through the fields were knee-deep in mud and the many riverlets and irrigation ditches were bridged by mud-covered plank bridges. All this had to be traversed in pitch darkness, weighed down with cloying mud, and heavy loads while listening to spent bullets hissing by. Enemy flare would cause the troops to 'freeze', with any movement attracting a hail of bullets. At a point just past the *Estaminet du Bon Coin* the enemy front trenches crossed the road,

The old road to Le Gheer showing Estaminet du Bon Coin. The front trench was about 50 yards behind the tree-line on the right. The road to the right led to the barricade.

shielded from view by a barricade. Another lane branched left at this barricade, following it for a while before crossing a long gap to another barricade, the carrying parties well aware that the German line was about 100 yards to their right. A little way along past this barricade, in a trench alongside the Le Gheer–Le Touquet road, was Company HQ where the parties would off-load and make their return. For some weeks HQ was out of contact with the front trench in daytime due to the flooded and unusable communication trenches. All reliefs were carried out by night for the same reason. During the day the troops in the line kept low to avoid being spotted by enemy snipers who fired on any target that suited them. If the troops did chance looking over the parapet, they would have seen no more than fields covered in wet mud and puddles, with no growth except stubby trees, and a mess of cans and empty tins thrown about near the trenches.

The front trench and trees the barricade side of the Estaminet du Bon Coin (seen at the crossroads in the distance). The photo was taken from the approximate position of the road barricade.

On 21 March the L.R.B. were back in Ploegsteert Wood taking over the 1st Somersets trenches and the left trench of the 1st Rifle Brigade. HQ was in *Rifle House* with the front split

A breastwork or barricade, which was garrisoned to keep the enemy at bay.

The type of view from over the parapet.

into three subsections, each manned by a company with supports in *Tourist Line* and *Hunter Avenue*, the fourth company being held in reserve in Ploegsteert village. Life was not too difficult in this sector, one of the battalion's duties being to escort V.I.Ps. along *Tourist Line* (from where they could claim to having 'been to the front'.

For those who could attend, Easter brought a welcome break when the Bishop of London visited, holding a service in the reserve billets and, on Easter Sunday, consecrating the L.R.B. burial plot south of Ploegsteert started by units of the 4th Division in December 1914.

On 18 April it went into rest at Steenwerck, the first rest since arriving in the line 5 months before. It now looked forward to a long break from the rigours of the front line, The weather was good, the billets were clean, sporting events had been arranged and prizes for the competitions had been bought – but good times were not to be. On 23 April, orders were received to move and, the following day, the battalion entrained for Poperinghe. From there it moved through Busseboom, Vlamertinghe, skirting north of Ypres to St Jean, then on to Wieltje and straight into the Second Battle of Ypres.

The L.R.B. stint at Ploegsteert was over and it would never return. The period it served there was unique in the sense that the village could not be considered to be in the back areas, it was virtually in the front line, and the troops manning that line billeted with the residents. The battalion enjoyed its time there and, likewise, the villagers had enjoyed the company of the 'Boutons Noirs' (Black Buttons) as they were known. Their attitude to civilians was different to that of the 'rough and ready' regulars, and the locals responded accordingly, opening their homes to them, sharing their hardships, and the grief of the battalion's casualties. The community made many friends in the L.R.B., friendships that lasted well into the future as the unveiling of a plaque in The London Rifle Brigade Cemetery would prove 12 years later.

On 19 June 1927 Lieutenant-General Sir H. F. M. Wilson, then late G. O. C. 4th Division, unveiled a tablet on a wall in the shelter at the entrance commemorating the cemetery's dedication (Easter Sunday

1915) and the L.R.B.'s fallen during the war. A parade was held in the village square and a Guard of Honour and the Regimental Band conducted a wreath-laying ceremony at Ploegsteert's war memorial, before setting off for the cemetery. The whole village turned out, with many old friendships renewed and every building was showing a flag, By the time the procession reached the cemetery, the road was blocked with spectators from Ploegsteert and its surrounding villages.

Many speeches were made during the unveiling by dignitaries, but the words probably appreciated most by the veterans and serving members of the regiment at the time were those finishing the speech by Lord Cairns, the battalion's wartime C.O. when he said:

> I like to picture future generations as they take their evening walks along the road which borders the cemetery, pointing, when they pass, to this gate with the words "There sleep the gentlemen of the Black Buttons"

After the unveiling ceremony, spectators and veterans alike visited the old front line, before the L.R.B. contingent left for England and Ploegsteert returned to its normal way of life.*

London Rifle Brigade Cemetery owes its name to the 21 casualties buried in Plot III during January to March of 1915, the first burial taking place on 12 January 1915 when the battalion was manning *Essex Trench.*

There are other cemeteries in the sector housing the graves of men from the L.R.B.: Lancashire Cottage Cemetery holds 7; Ploegsteert Wood Military Cemetery 10, and Rifle House Cemetery just one.

Perhaps the most touching story of all the men who fell in the sector is that of Riflemen Jack Dunnet, the battalion's first casualty whose grave was lost in the wood. His name is commemorated on the Ploegsteert Memorial to the Missing, the only member of the London Rifle Brigade remembered on that memorial.**

Today's Ploegsteert community have not forgotten those who fell in the Great War, L.R.B. or otherwise. Every year, Armistice Day is a local holiday with a ceremony held at the Ploegsteert Memorial, two marathons (8km and 16km) being run by competitors from all over Europe, a fairground is enjoyed in the village square and cafés and restaurants are open well into the night. Throughout the year school children are encouraged to learn of the events of the 1914-18 period and, at 7 pm on the first Friday of every month of the year, *Last Post* is sounded at the Ploegsteert Memorial complemented with dedicated readings and the laying of wreaths by a multitude of individuals and associations.

The London Rifle Brigade can make claim to the fact that those many 'Black Buttons' of its 1st Battalion who lie at rest in the area started all that activity in today's Ploegsteert.

*See Appendix A, page 106.

**See Appendix B, page 107.

The London Rifle Brigade Cemetery in the early post war years.

Children carrying wreaths in the parade to the London Rifle Brigade Cemetery.

The scene at the unveiling of the Memorial Plaque in 1927.

Notes:

1. The 'Brigade' designation was only allowed if a Corps comprised at least two battalions and was to be used by the London unit against the clear understanding that its complement would be increased to 1,000 in the shortest possible time.

2. Although the oldest of London's volunteer units, the authority determining the structure of the newly formed London defence forces designated precedence in seniority to four Royal Fusilier battalions, a decision not well received by the L.R.B.

3. The 2nd London Brigade comprised: 1/5th (City of London) Regiment (The London Rifle Brigade); 1/6th (City of London) Regiment (Rifles); 1/7th (City of London) Regiment and 1/8th (City of London) Regiment (Post Office Rifles).

4. The Benedictine Convent was later to find fame as the GHQ Machine Gun School.

5. 11th Brigade, 4th Division was made up of: 1st Somerset Light Infantry; 1st East Lancashire Regiment; 1st Hampshire Regiment and 1st Rifle Brigade.

6. 18-year old Rifleman Jack L. Dunnett, whose grave was lost in later shelling, is commemorated on the Ploegsteert Memorial, Panel 10.

7. Bunter Avenue, was renamed Bunhill Row by the L.R.B. after the London street which houses its HQ.

8. *Essex Farm*, was a moated farm on clearing in Ploegsteert Wood edging the Ploegsteert-Le Gheer road, not to be confused with *Essex House* on the road leading from the Ploegsteert-Armentières road to the Estaminet de Bon Coin. Today *Essex Farm* is no longer there, but traces of its moat are still evident.

9. The breastworks of mud, logs and sandbags, constructed in sections about 50 yards apart, were a substitute for trenches – tree roots made trenches impossible to dig – and the watershed caused any diggings to fill immediately with water. Pillboxes later built along Hunter Avenue, were described by Anthony Eden, future Prime Minister of Great Britain who served in the wood with the 21st KRRC in 1916, as "... a series of unimpressive forts offering no protection from shellfire".

10. L/Cpl M. Roach was killed while the battalion was consolidating the position. He is buried in Rifle House Cemetery Plot IV, Row F, Grave 8.

11. The Christmas Truce of 1914 had a lasting influence on a young rifleman then serving with the battalion. Henry Williamson, later to become a famous author, his *Tarka the Otter* and his series of books entitled *Chronicles of Ancient Sunlight* becoming particularly well known, was left with feelings of disgust and the belief that Britain and Germany should never have been at war and should certainly never go to war with each other again. In the 30s he attended the National Socialist Congress at Nuremberg and was impressed with the Hitler Youth movement. He joined Oswald Mosley's British Union of Fascists and due to his political views was briefly interned at the beginning of World War Two.

12. The Warnave flowed east to west and vice versa subject to wind direction. An official map at the time named it 'The River Warnave or Mckenna' after the politician R. McKenna, a Liberal MP. He was Home Secretary (1911-15), Chancellor of the Exchequer in Asquith's coalition (1915-16) and resigned when David Lloyd George displaced Asquith as Prime Minister.

Appendix A

The following are comments made by various members of the London Rifle Brigade following their visit to Ploegsteert for the unveiling of the commemorative plaque in The London Rifle Brigade Cemetery on June 28 1927:

"Nearly 400 members of the London Rifle Brigade attended the unveiling of a memorial tablet in the L.R.B. cemetery at Ploegsteert yesterday. The ceremony was performed by Lieut.-General Sir H. F. M. Wilson.

The little village of " Plug Street," as it was always known to the troops, was gaily beflagged in honour of the "Black Buttons"—the name by which we riflemen were known to the villagers."

"To those who had spent the winter of 1914 and the spring of 1915 in the village it was a day dedicated to old memories, but those who hoped to recognise old landmarks were destined to disappointment.

Plug Street, like the other villages along the front, after being reduced to a heap of brick dust, has been so completely rebuilt as to become unrecognisable even to those of us who knew its geography as well as we know our own suburb.

But there was no mistaking our old friends among the villagers as we passed through the thronged streets. There was the genial host of the Estaminet Des Trois Amis outside his rebuilt home, there was the buxom proprietor of the cake-shop, and standing beside her Maurice, her grown-up son, whom we had known as a little boy. Round the corner my billet lady waited with the baby daughter I used to dangle on my knee, now grown a good-looking flapper."

"In the afternoon Ploegsteert Wood was full of familiar faces, searching for familiar spots, many of which were easily found. The barricades were there. Tourist Avenue and Tourist Peep, Hunter Avenue and Bunhill Row, overgrown and untrodden as they are now were nevertheless fairly recognisable. These, and the graves in our own cemetery and those in Rifle House cemetery in the Wood combined to awaken memories of which each one must be left to speak for himself."

"But it was up in Plug Street Wood, where formerly we had known every tree, where we had dug, and built, and carried burdens, that we were most completely at sea. Trenches and barricades had almost disappeared in a tangled mass of brambles and undergrowth."

"It took us a whole afternoon's diligent search to locate the probable position of Bunhill Row, of Piccadilly Circus, Hyde Park Corner, Hunter Avenue.

Thirteen years ago, when we shovelled what felt like half Flanders into sand-bags to build Bunhill Row, we thought we were changing the face of the earth. To-day, except for a stray sheet of corrugated iron, and a few rusty bits of barbed wire hidden beneath the wild roses, there is no trace of our handiwork. But for a stray shell here and there and the few scarred tree stumps which the Belgian foresters have not yet cut down, there is no sign of war, until through the trees you perceive in a clearing the white tombstones of those who fell."

Appendix B

As many people were heard to ask why the grave of Pte. J. L. Dunnett in Rifle House Cemetery at Ploegsteert was marked by a wooden cross and not by a headstone, the following correspondence with the Imperial War Graves Commission on the subject is published.

June 27, 1927
The Secretary, The War Graves Commission, Baker Street, W.I.
DEAR SIR,
When visiting "Rifle House" Cemetery in Ploegsteert Wood on Sunday, June 19 last I noticed that the grave of Pte. J. L. Dunnett of the London Rifle Brigade was marked by what appeared to be the original wooden cross and not by the head-stone of the usual pattern.

Pte. Dunnett was the first member of the London Rifle Brigade to be killed in action (November 20, 1914), and I should be greatly obliged if you would inform me if there is any reason for the distinction in the marking of his grave.

The visit, on which I was one of a party of four hundred members and friends of the Regiment, was for the purpose of unveiling a memorial tablet in the London Rifle Brigade Cemetery at Ploegsteert, and in the course of our visit we viewed many cemeteries in the Ypres and Ploegsteert sectors. I would like to say that on every hand I heard expressions of appreciation and great gratitude for the beautiful state in which our cemeteries are being kept.
Yours very truly,
F. P. BARRY,
Captain and Editor, L.R.B. RECORD.

The following reply was received :—
War Graves Commission
82 Baker Street, London W.I.
July 6, 1927.

SIR,
With reference to your letter of the 27th ult, I very much regret that no in-formation has been received regarding the burial-place of Rifleman J. L. Dunnett.
The battle areas have been searched, and the remains of all those soldiers who were buried in isolated or scattered graves have been removed and re-buried but the name of this soldier has not appeared on the reports of this work.

As you will understand in many areas military operations caused the destruction of crosses and graves registration marks, and completely changed the surface of the ground, so that the work of identifying even those graves of which the position was accurately known has often been extremely difficult.

I am very sorry not to be able to send you a more satisfactory reply. I am to add that the cross erected in Rifle House Cemetery upon which Rifle-man J. L. Dunnett's name appears is a temporary memorial only, and memorials of this nature are not replaced by permanent stones.

I am to say that as it has unfortunately not been possible to locate this soldier's grave, his name will be commemorated on a memorial which the Commission propose to erect in the neighbourhood of Ploegsteert to the memory of soldiers who gave their lives in the late War, and whose graves it has not been possible to identify. I am, Sir,
Your obedient Servant,
T. J. BLAKER,
for Principal Assistant Secretary.

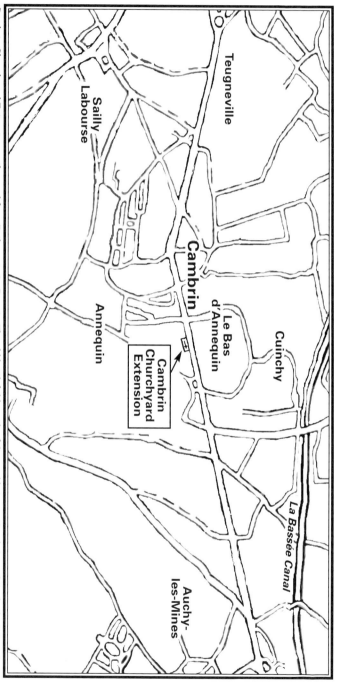

Cambrin Churchyard Extension on the road from Bethune to La Bassee. The old battlefield south of the road between Cambrin and Auchy-les-Mines is as bare of buildings as it was in 1915, the area now a large expanse of well cultivated open fields where was once a network of opposing trench systems studded with masses of shellholes. (See map on page 110)

Where our best
Sustained the strife of war
When hopes were at their lowest
Pindar.

10
THE BRAVEST OF THE BRAVE
Captain A. L. Samson M.C.
2nd Battalion Royal Welch Fusiliers
The Battle of loos, 25 September 1915

THE BRAVEST OF THE BRAVE is an overworked phrase that students of the Great War years of 1914-18 will often encounter, so much so that its true meaning is diluted. However, there is one who fits this noble profile lying quietly in a soldier's grave in the Cambrin Churchyard Extension situated just off the old wartime highway that links Béthune and La Bassée. The cemetery houses 1,112 British burials and is noted for the large number grouped in battalions with headstones carrying the date 25 September 1915, the first day of the Battle of Loos.[1]

Capt. A L Samson M.C.

Amongst the grouping of the 2nd Royal Welch Fusiliers lays Captain Arthur Legge Samson M.C., who was killed in the opening phase of the battle while commanding the battalion's C Company. Awarded the Military Cross for gallantry and leadership earlier in 1915, he seems to epitomise all that is inherent in the description *The Bravest of the Brave*.[2]

On the 25th he was in the line in the Cuinchy/Cambrin sector south of La Bassée Canal. His regiment, together with the 1st Middlesex, 2nd Argyll & Sutherland Highlanders and 1st Cameronions, part of 19th Brigade, 2nd Division were about to play their part in the Battle of Loos – the objective of which was the capture of a vital area of German defences west of the town of Lens, and so assist French military efforts further south in the Artois region.[3]

The 2nd Division's overall objective in the opening phase was to:

... attack and occupy the enemy's front trenches opposite Givenchy from the left of the 9th Division to the La Bassée Canal. Subsidiary attack: the left brigade of the 2nd Division holding the line north of the canal – the enemy's trenches opposite Givenchy and to push on to the line Chapelle St. Roch–Canteleux...

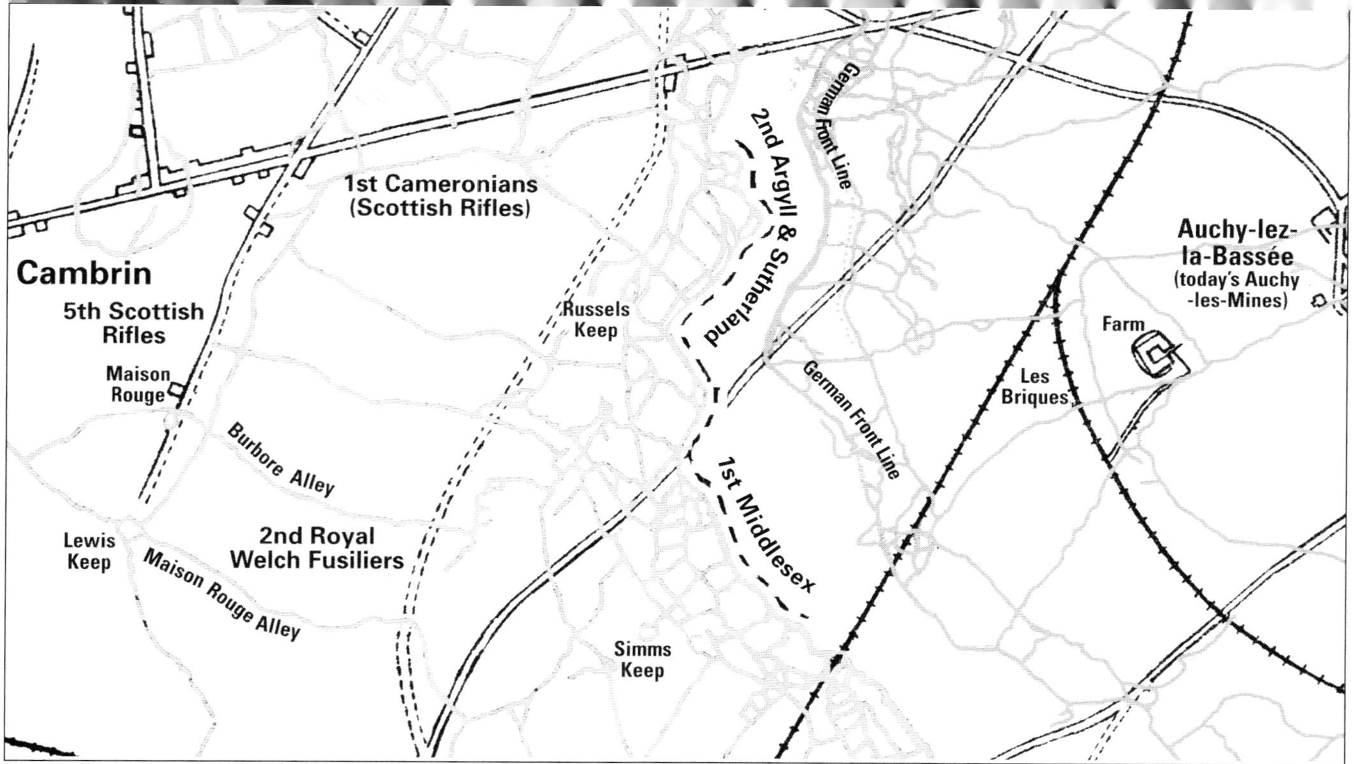

Cambrin

5th Scottish Rifles

Maison Rouge

Lewis Keep

Maison Rouge Alley

Burbure Alley

2nd Royal Welch Fusiliers

1st Cameronians (Scottish Rifles)

Russels Keep

Simms Keep

1st Middlesex

2nd Argyll & Sutherland

German Front Line

German Front Line

Les Briques

Farm

Auchy-lez-la-Bassée
(today's Auchy
-les-Mines)

The positions of the 19th Brigade battalions in the French-built trench system south of La Bassée Canal and forward of Cambrin on the morning of 25 September 1915.

110

The main and subsidiary attacks will be prepared by a bombardment commencing 21st September...

The Brigade's attack would launch from a French-built trench system forward of Cambrin just south of La Bassée Canal towards the village of Auchy-lez-la-Bassée (rebaptised after the war as today's Auchy-les-Mines) and the formidable defensive position called the *Hohenzollern Redoubt* with its defensive slag heaps and craters.

The battalion's order-of-battle was, in the front-line trenches from left to right, the 2nd Argyll & Sutherland Highlanders (supported by the 1st Cameronian (Scottish Rifles) and the 1st Middlesex (supported by the 2nd Welch Fusiliers). In reserve: 5th Scottish Rifles.

Men of B and C Companies, 2nd Royal Welch were pleased enough to have been allotted the task of supporting the 1st Middlesex, the two battalions having forged a close kinship through being under fire together in several previous actions.[4]

The overall picture presented by the plan of battle to the infantry troops involved was of a:

... short, intensive artillery bombardment during which the gas was to be released making all the enemy casualties. The leading battalions would then stroll across to the enemy lines and proceed to occupy an orchard about 1,000 yards distant.

Asphyxiating gas (Chlorine) was to be used for the first time by the British to assist in the attack. It was to be released at 5.50 am on the day and left to do its damage over the enemy lines before the infantry attack launched at 6.30 am. At the same time as the gas cylinders were activated, the supports, B Company (commanded by Captain Samson) and C company in the case of the Royal Welch, would move forward and form up in the front line trenches about 200 yards ahead, just as the last of the front line troops were leaving them to open the attack. All this while under the "short, intensive artillery bombardment" on the enemy front line.

At 1.00 am on the 25th, Captain Samson led his company into the cramped, French style of deep assembly trenches in front of Cambrin,

each man carrying a rifle with fixed bayonet, 200 rounds of S.A.A., extra rations, a pick or shovel or other tools, and a number of them with an issue of new type of hand grenade.[5] As if this were not enough, adding to their discomfort every man wore a P.H. Gas Helmet on his head, ready to roll-down to his

Front and side views of a 'rolled-down' P.H. Gas Helmet.

shoulders at a moment's notice, and, on top of the helmet was balanced his cap, the whole held in place with a piece of string tied below his chin,

As planned, the gas was released on time and the support companies left their trenches, heading for the front. They came under heavy shelling immediately as, during the time waiting to go over the top, German artillery had started to pummel the British front line and communication trenches. Added to this, the release of the gas in this sector had proved disastrous. Unfavourable wind conditions caused it to drift from left to right across the line and to fall back into the trenches along the 2nd Division's front causing many of the front line troops to suffer gas inhalation. Fortunately, their death rate was minimal, but nevertheless many were disabled by it and unable to take part in the attack.[6] Much to the consternation of many British officers at the number of casualties this caused, the attack went forward.[7]

The ground in front of the advancing infantry was already dotted with craters resulting from previous mine warfare in the area. Two mines blown by 173rd Tunnelling Company ten minutes before zero hour, had the secondary effect of putting the enemy on full alert. Consequentially, apart from moving under heavy shellfire, the advancing infantry were forced to bunch together to find its way around these craters, and suffered many of the troops being hit by concentrated machine gun and rifle fire as they did so.

The German front line troops had been withdrawn to their support lines during most of the British bombardment and had returned to their trenches with a vengeance, standing shoulder-to-shoulder on their fire steps, firing at will and taking a heavy toll of the advancing British.[8] This, together with the accurate shelling took its toll on the

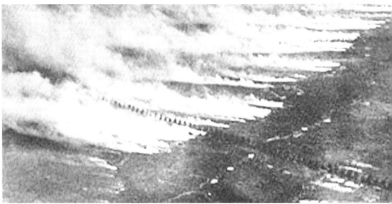

Chlorine gas released from cylinders,

already diminished attack force making it clear to all concerned that the 19th Brigade's attempts to meet its objectives was failing.

By 9.00 am it was obvious that no progress was going to be made, and Brigade Command gave orders to withdraw to the original front lines. Troops of the 1st Middlesex were in no position to withdraw because of the concentrated fire across No-Man's land and took whatever cover the could until dark. Some men of the 2nd Argyll & Sutherland Highlanders occupied an empty German trench, but only 11 returned at night, the rest having been killed or captured.

In the meantime, the support companies had been making slow headway in the communication trenches caused by jams brought about by heavy shelling, trench damage, runners, stretcher-bearers and the walking wounded making their way back. Nevertheless, both companies finally made it to the front line trench finding it occupied by the dead and wounded, with the gas, still drifting back causing many of the helpless wounded to experience further suffering. In front of the trench the troops were to see the ground ahead littered with the dead and wounded Middlesex, with those wounded who could, making efforts to crawl back to their line.

At about 8 o'clock, although any form of success was no more than an over-ambitious hope, whistles were blown and Captain Samson and his company went over the top to join what was left of the 1st Middlesex still fighting desperately for survival at the *Railway*

British infantry advancing through a gas cloud during the opening of the Battle of Loos.

Redoubt, situated just in front of the village of Auchy-les-La Bassée. There were no shells falling on the German line opposite when the supports advanced, the morning was bright and clear, and the enemy riflemen and machine gunners opposite, now finding more British troops to target, settled themselves in to an undisturbed killing frenzy.

Samson, leading his company in a courageous attempt to reach the Middlesex line, only covered a distance of about 40 yards before he was hit several times and fell, as did many of his men. B Company to its right had fallen after 30 yards. The support attack faulted and petered out.

So ended Captain Samson's life in an action that was flawed from its outset. As one brother officer quoted to another in his summing up of the action:

> ... mismanagement at the top, inefficiency in the middle, want of training at the bottom.

Poet and Author Robert Graves,[9] who knew and served with Samson in the battalion, recorded his account of that part of the action in his classic book, *Goodbye to all That*:

> A few minutes later Captain Samson, with C Company and the remainder of B Company reached our front line. Finding the trench full of dying men, he decided to go over too. He could not have it said that the Royal Welsh had let down the Middlesex. A strong comradely feeling bound both regiments, so he attacked with the parts of the two companies he had.

He continues:

> My mouth was dry, my eyes out of focus, and my legs quaking under me I found a water bottle full of rum, and drank about half a pint, it quieted me, and my head remained clear. Samson was lying wounded about twenty yards away from the front trench. Several attempts were made to get him in. He was very badly hit and groaning. Three men were killed in these attempts, and two officers and two men wounded. Finally his own orderly managed to crawl out to him. Samson ordered him back, saying that he was riddled and not worth rescuing; he sent his apologies to the company for making such a noise...

> ... At dusk, when the firing had relented, we all went out to get in the wounded, leaving only the sentries in the line. The first body I came upon was Samson... hit in seventeen places. I found that he had forced his knuckles into his mouth to stop himself crying out with the pain and attracting any more of his men to their death.

Graves also dedicated one of his works to the Captain in tribute. His poem, *The Dead Fox Hunter, In Memory of Captain L. Samson* was written about this battle:

> *We found the little Captain at the head. His men lay well aligned. We touched his hand - stone cold dead. And they all dead behind.*

Captain Samson M.C. was most certainly one of those who clearly saw and honoured his duty on 25 September 1915.

And so he died, as so many others did on that tragic day, feeling quite cut-off from all humanity. His passing though was one of a classic nobility in the highest sense. He was very much missed by his men and his brother officers alike who recognised in him one who could truly regale in that simple title *The Bravest of the Brave.*

Mention made by a Lieutenant H. M. Blair gives an indication of the worth of the man when, in the days immediately before the attack, active patrolling to check the enemy wire was the order of the day:

> Samson, who was always relieved to know that anyone in his command these days was not married, sent me with a corporal and a bomber to check the German wire ...

He lies today close to where he fell, in Cambrin Churchyard Extension, barely one mile from the battle lines. He is among his own men, and the fallen of the Middlesex Regiment whom he had so bravely tried to assist in his last hours.

May he, and all of them, truly Rest in Peace.

Cambrin Churchyard Extension.

Notes:

1. 2 miles west of Cuinchy and 5 miles east of Béthune, the Cambrin Churchyard Extension holds 1,211 British, 150 French and 3 German burials. It features a very large number of graves grouped by battalion, the most predominant being 79 of the 2nd Argyll and Sutherland Highlanders and 15 of the 1st Cameronians in Row C, and 35 of the 2nd Royal Welch Fusiliers and 115 of the 1st Middlesex in Row H, all dating from 25 September 1915.

2. Captain Arthur Legge Samson was born 1 June 1882 at Oxford Terrace, Paddington, London. Educated at Eton and Merton College, Oxford. He enlisted in the 2nd Battalion Royal Welch Fusiliers at war's outbreak and was awarded the Military Cross on 23 June 1915 for his conduct in an action in the La Bassée Canal sector. He is buried in Row K. Grave 20 of the Cambrin Churchyard Extension

3. The French Field Marshal Joffre, developed an offensive with the objective of breaking the German lines in the Champagne Valley, Artois, and Loos – the Loos offensive to be taken on the British First Army. By 28 September, the Battle of Loos was over and the British had suffered 60,000 casualties having been taught a hard-earned lesson in what their first real offensive action in the Great War.

8 October saw the Third Battle of Artois and Second Battle of Champagne finished. The French lost control of the British forces and General Haig replaced General French as the Commander-in-Chief of the British Army.

4. Robert Graves comments on the Royal Welch's kinship with the 1st Middlesex as: "... they were drawn together in their dislike for the Scots or 'Jocks' in the Argyll and Sutherland."

5. The new type hand grenades were of a "ball" pattern, and had to be ignited from a kind of match-box striker strapped to the wrist of the bomber, but the damp atmosphere and the falling rain on 25 September 1915 made ignition impossible.

6. British gas casualties numbered 2,632 but only seven died through it. The gas [Chlorine] was released from cylinders in a specially devised trench in front of the main front-line trenches housing the troops. Smoke was activated at the same time to help thicken the gas cloud and so help screen the Infantry in their forward move.

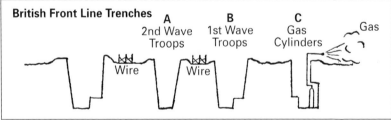

British Front Line Trenches
A
2nd Wave Troops
Wire
B
1st Wave Troops
Wire
C
Gas Cylinders
Gas

7. The Brigadier asked to have the gas order cancelled on the 19th Brigade front but was informed it was "too late".

8. The 1st Middlesex lost over 450 men and the A & S Highlanders lost 330.

9. Robert Graves was reputed by his brother officers to have "... the largest feet in the army", The Battle of Loos was his first real experience of war which resulted in only 5 company officers of the battalion surviving. His described what he saw of the 2nd Division's sector of the battle as "a bloody balls-up".

The Man in White

Many an hour I had lain in pain.
Through scorching heat to frozen night,
When from afar across the shattered waste,
I saw at first The Man in White.

I felt my life blood ebb away,
And in my agony went my failing sight.
But my heart did pound with a strength renewed
As I saw come closer The Man in White.

He heeded not the roaring guns,
Or the sounds of terror in that awful night.
But he brought with him his love and care,
That was the message of The Man in White

I knew not who my new friend was,
Only that he would relieve my plight.
My bleeding hands went out to his,
I saw the gentle eyes of The Man in White.

"Follow me friend, and I'll take you home"
His voice so soft in the brilliant light.
And he took me from this painful world,
I followed him thus, The Man in White.

T. Spagnoly 2000

The Ypres Town Cemetery and Extension at the corner of the Menin Road and the Zonnebeke Road, a short walk along Maarschalk Frenchlaan from the Menin Gate, and well worth the visit.

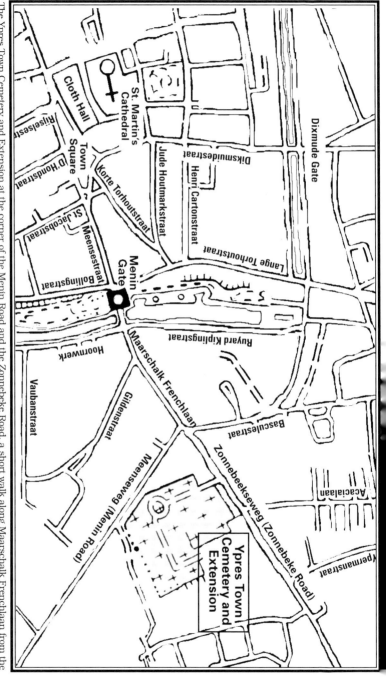

Blow out, you bugles, over the rich Dead!
Rupert Brooke

11
INTERLUDE AT YPRES
Ypres Town Cemetery and Extension,
Menin Road, Ypres.

THERE are many British Military Cemeteries in and around Ypres where the visitor can seek the appropriate time of quiet contemplation that these places of sacrifice deserve. One such place, encompassing two cemeteries, has the perfect profile for such moments. The Ypres Town Cemetery and Extension certainly demand a visit by all those who attend the evening tribute of *Last Post* sounded nightly at the nearby Menin Gate.

Wedged as they are in the fork between the roads, the once dreaded Menin Road leading to Hooge, and that equally as frightening road leading to Zonnebeke and Passchendaele, names that will forever ring heavy with the tones of sacrifice, duty and loyalty. There are no better places to induce a reflective mood.

It is here that the visior can find the paradox of life and death in close proximity, where the graves of British soldiers are almost in the back gardens of private dwellings with children playing and the day's normal domestic existence being played out – a perfect co-existence – the peace the local community enjoy today being the legacy left by those who fell. Whenever he came to Ypres, this was usually the first cemetery he visited.

He was struck by the fact that the cemetery registers showed that no visits were recorded from between three and four weeks, and that generally, visitors are few and far between – strange when considering the thousands of people who attend the Menin Gate ceremony just a short stroll away. Do they begrudge the few hundred-metre walk up Maarshalk Frenchlaan, the sloping road leading to the cemetery's enclosures and the Menin Road itself?[1] Odd if that is the case, seeing that the theme of remembrance is what caused their visit to the town in the first place. Maybe they do not know of the existence of the cemetery so close to where they stand as they listen to the haunting sound generated by the Ypres buglers.

Those men lying so close deserve to be remembered ... they gave their all, and it takes very little effort to recognise it.

The Menin Gate in March 1915 looking from Rue de Menin [today's Frenchlaan] across the bridge spanning the ramparts' moat.

The Ypres Town Cemetery itself was used by the British in 1914 until February 1915 and once again in 1918. It houses the graves of 144 British soldiers and one of the Indian Army who fell in the Great War.

Sited just east of the Town Cemetery, the Ypres Town Cemetery Extension was begun in 1914 and used until April of 1915 and, on two occasions, in 1918 amounting to 215 burials.

After the Armistice, the Extension was expanded by the Concentration of 367 graves from small cemeteries and isolated graves east and northeast of Ypres. It was used for military burials in a later war also, housing 43 graves of men who died in the Second World War, most of them casualties from when General Montgomery's 3rd Division fought a rearguard action to protect the withdrawal of the British Expeditionary Force to the Channel ports of Calais and Dunkirk in 1940.[2]

A different war perhaps, but the same sacrifice by men of the same nations against the same foe.

The Extension is always so peaceful in the early evening as the light begins to fade, and before the bugles begin their sad refrain. The visitors, if and when they do come, will have much to appreciate when strolling between the headstones inscribed with their fair share of heart-tugging inscriptions.

One in particular: '*He was everyones friend*' always prompted him to think what a delightful saying with which to enter eternity. Private P. Flannagan, 7/8th Battalion, King's Own Scottish Borderers, was killed on 31 July 1917, the opening day of the Third Battle of Ypres. He is still 'Believed to be buried' in the cemetery with his special memorial in the last headstone in Plot III, Row B, right up against the cemetery boundary, a few feet away from the garden of the house behind it. Has he ever had a visitor to himself? ... he could easily have one on a daily basis, and with so little effort, and he was going to have one this day.

The mother of 34-year old Private Johnstone Macpherson, 1st Battalion, Black Watch, had inscribed on her son's headstone in Plot II, Row A, Grave 11: '*My son died by a strangers hand, his limbs reposed*'. Mother and son had been reunited these many years, a comforting thought. He had died up near Polygon Wood on 1 November 1914 at the end of the First Battle of Ypres, but would he have survived the following four years of bloodshed? The odds would have weighed heavily against him.

'*I think of him in silence, No one may see me weep. But deep within my heart, his memory I will keep*' marks the memory of Private R. C. Coomber in Plot II, Row A, Grave 51, killed in action on 27 October

The Menin Gate today.

1914 with the 1st Battalion, The Queen's (Royal West Surrey Regiment) and Grave 52, that of 36-year old Private D. Campbell, 1st Battalion, Cameron Highlanders who died of his wounds on 28 October 1914. Both had died before the Salient had even evolved. Had the fates been kind to them in taking them so early?

He always made a point of standing a for a little while by Sergeant Thomas Payne's grave in Plot III, Row C. What sadness and grief his family must have experienced when being informed of his death, just a few months after they had learned, and been being happy in the knowledge, that he had survived the war? Serving with the 2nd Australian Light Railway Operating Company, he had died of accidental injuries on 23 February 1919,

How many of the men lying here had wearily trudged up that slope from the old Menin Gate taking one of those two dreaded roads past the town's communal cemetery, wet, hungry, tired, and dispirited, weighed down with heavy loads to meet their fate and destiny further up in the line? Had they known of the work then going on in the civilian cemetery alongside the road to Zonnebeke preparing an

Ypres Town Cemetery Extension with the gardens of domestic dwellings back-to-back with the cemetery boundary.

extension to house a military burial plot for some of the wretched soles amongst them, the bodies that would be carried back by grieving comrades to a final resting place a few days later?

It does not take much of a leap of imagination to picture the scene of suffering humanity in the shadows of today's fast-flowing motorised traffic passing the suburban shops, cafes and domestic dwellings where the road and house lights flicker on with the onset of evening ... talk about living with ghosts. Somehow the noisy two-way traffic does not seem at odds with the peacefully dignity of the orderly rows of military headstones.

A pity that those who are so moved by the ceremony at the Menin Gate back along that down-sloping road don't make the effort to follow just a little in the footsteps of those who passed before them so many years before.

"Time is ever the thief" they say. Well, it steals and passes very quickly at this place he said to himself. A pity, there is so much to see and so little of that precious time to see it..

How could anyone have such a trivial thought at such a place as this he wondered, but he knew he couldn't cope with high octane sentiment and emotion twenty four hours a day. He had to get his feet back to earth sometimes.

Ypres was a place that seared deeply into the British psyche and should forever be so. Sir Winston Churchill who had served in Flanders in the sector south of Ypres had uttered memorably:" *A more sacred place to the British nation did not exist in the world*".

A sentiment most would agree with.

The Cemetery Extension houses some notable graves which lends it a unique character. The aristocracy are represented here along with the humble of the land.

Lord Charles Sackville Pelham Worsley, a machine gun officer with the Royal Horse

The Household Cavalry memorial at Zandvoorde on the site of Lord Worsley's original grave where he was buried by the Germans.

Lieut. Lord Worsley, Royal Horse Guards

The marker erected by the Worsley family to replace the original one placed to mark the grave by the Germans.

Guards, 7th Cavalry Brigade is buried here in Plot II, Row D, Grave.

He was killed whilst manning his machine guns during the heavy fighting at Zandvoorde on 31 October 1914 and was initially buried by the enemy, his grave being located after the Armistice from a sketch provided by them.

The Household Cavalry memorial at Zandvoorde is constructed over the actual site of his first grave. His body was recovered in the early post war years and was reburied with full military honours here in 1922.

In Plot III, Row AA are the graves of some of the staff of General Haig's 1st Corps who were in conference at the Hooge Château annexe along the Menin Road, then being used as the joint Headquarters of the British 1st and 2nd Divisions, on 31 October 1914 at a particularly critical time during the First Battle of Ypres.

Major-Generals Lomax and Monro, General Officer Commanding

Lord Worsley's funeral cortege on its way to the Ypres Town Extension Cemetery.

1st and 2nd Divisions respectively, were holding discussions there when, at 1.15 pm German artillery laid down a heavy barrage on the Château registering a few direct hits which caused a great deal of chaos and killed a number of the two divisional staffs. General Munro was stunned and reduced to a state of shock and General Lomax was seriously injured, later dying of his wounds in England in 1915.

This could have had a serious affect on the ongoing conduct of the battle at such a vitally balanced time, but Field Marshal Haig realigned his command staff, and finally won the day, withholding the prize of Ypres from the grasp of the Kaiser. The casualties from the annexe shelling buried in Plot III, Row AA are:

Grave 2 – 43-year old Lieutenant-Colonel Arthur Jax Blake Percival, D.S.O., Northumberland Fusiliers and 2nd Division Staff;

Grave 3 – 42-year old Major George Paley, Rifle Brigade and 1st Division Staff;

Grave 4 – 47-year old Colonel Frederic Walter Kerr, D.S.O. 1st Battalion Gordon Highlanders, 1st Division H.Q.

Grave 5 – 36-year old Major Francis Maxwell Chenevix-Trench, 2nd Division Staff, Royal Field Artillery.

Grave 6 – Captain Rupert Ommanney, Royal Engineers and 2nd Division Staff.

In the same row with those ranking officers of 1st Corps, is Gunner

The Hooge Château annexe after the direct hit from enemy shelling.

W. Marchant, 35th Heavy Battery, Royal Garrison Artillery who also died on 31 October.

Gunner Marchant, buried in Grave 1 of this plot, takes 'pride of place', in Row AA, but why would he be buried at the beginning of the row sectioned for those Divisional Staff Officers? Maybe the clue lays with Captain Graham Percival Shedden, also of 35th Heavy Battery, Royal Garrison Artillery, who died later in the day from the wounds he received during the shelling of the Hooge Château annexe. He is buried, not in the Extension, but in a military plot close to the far corner of the perimeter wall. Gunner Marchant could have been Shedden's batman, his driver, or both.

Whatever the case he and the senior officers resting alongside are a fine example of the Commonwealth War Graves Commission's principle of equality in death amongst all ranks.

Plot III, Row A carries the graves of 19 of the men and women of the Commonwealth War Graves Commission who had died naturally after a service of dedication and duty to the many fallen. They lay under pseudo-military style headstones after a lifetime of service, duly remembered for, and in recognition of, their contribution to the commendable work carried out in the immediate post war years ... and so they should be. It was due to them and all the others involved with the work of the Commission that some rudimentary order was brought to the tangled mess of the battlefields, resulting in the orderly aspects that we visit and enjoy today. Others civilians who worked

King George V (left) with Marshal Foch (third from left) and other British and French dignitaries in the 20s at the Ypres Town Cemetery plot near the perimeter wall.

Plot III. Row A. The graves of the 19 men and women of the Commonwealth War Graves Commission.

with the Commission lie with similar headstones in the community plots of the older Ypres Town Cemetery itself.

Leaving the Extension through the exit at the far end of the cemetery, he wandered into this older Ypres Town Cemetery stopping just inside to rest a while at the grave of another aristocrat, Lieutenant H. H. Prince Maurice Victor Donald of Battenburg K.C.V.O., 1st Battalion King's Royal Rifle Corps. Grandson of Queen Victoria, he was mortally wounded in an attack toward the Keiburg Spur east of Broodseinde Ridge in October 1914.

At least, he thought. this early exit from the proceedings had spared the young Prince from the horrors and obscenities that would befall so many of his generation in the succeeding years. The Prince's grave, although registered in the Ypres Town Cemetery, is royally set aside close to the wall near the entrance of the Extension but, as with all British military graves, it features the uniform military headstone that identifies all the fallen in the Great War, no matter what title, rank, honour, class or creed.

Noisy traffic outside the cemetery, and the sounds of children playing in the neighbouring garden by the footpath exit jolted him

The Ypres Town Cemetery civilian plot with the CWGC members' military style headstones.

23-year old Lieut. H. H. Prince Maurice of Battenburg.

from his moodful reverie ... time to go, he shivered as the evening chill suddenly hit him. The noise of the children had alerted him to the lateness of the hour. The crowds and bugles would soon be assembling at the nearby Menin Gate. Nearly time to leave the cemeteries. A final glance at the grave of Private Macpherson and his mother's heart-tugging inscription which always brought tears to his eyes, much as he tried not to be so affected by the grieving kin of a lifetime ago - but some hit home and remain, This one hurt, as it always did.

He experienced the usual call on his emotions standing there, knowing that he would be experiencing more of them when he left to join others assembling at the Menin Gate. He had gone through this so many times before: a visit to the cemeteries; then a stroll to the Gate; a short wait; then a few moments of anticipation before the soulful notes of *Last Post* sailed out over the old Ypres Salient, encompassing all those lost hopes, extinguished in mud and fire, that will forever lie there having taken a nation's potential with them.

Closing the gate quietly behind him in the gathering gloom. Why did

King George V visiting the grave of Prince Maurice of Battenburg in May 1922.

he do that here he wondered? It was not as if he was going to wake anyone. The children had already been called in. The lights were on in the houses, providing a scene of peaceful domesticity, the families enjoying their evening meals or watching television – their peace purchased with the blood of the many Britons who would lie forever almost in their back gardens. It was a perfect paradox, and it seemed right somehow, and calmed his mental agitation as he stepped outside onto the Zonnebeke road, now gearing up with the evening traffic heading for the Ypres Town Square and its attendant pleasures. Who could blame them for that. The war and its suffering is just a part of history to most of the inhabitants of Ypres. As a close Flemish friend had said in recent years: "You must not be a dinosaur about times past. The new currency to the young Yprois is jobs and housing". It made sense when he thought about it. This is the price paid and the legacy left by the men who all lie in and around the old town. He couldn't argue with the wisdom of it. He shouldn't live in the past. He had to move forward.

He headed for the Menin Gate knowing full well that, when he came back to Ypres again, his thoughts and feeling would be exactly the same as they were on this visit.

The grave of Prince Maurice of Battenburg after the war.

Notes.

1. The Maarschalk Frenchlaan section of the road leading from the Ypres Town Square to the Menin Gate was originally the beginning of the Menin Road. It was re-named in the post war years after Field Marshal French, Commander in Chief British Expeditionary Force (BEF) 1914.

2. The fighting around Ypres in 1940 stemming the German movement towards the coast was in defence of the canal system around the town costing the British around 700 men. The wounded were cared for in three civilian hospitals in Ypres: Hospital de Notre Dame, The Clinique Soeur Noires and the Red Cross Hospital in St Aloisius School in D'Hondstraat. Those who died in these hospital were buried in the Town Cemetery Extension. Others who had been buried where they fell were later moved to the Extension together with two who were first buried in the civilian section of the town cemetery.

3. The nephew of Prince Maurice of Battenburg, the cousin of Queen Elizabeth II, became Supreme Allied Commander in the Far East during the Second World War, his name anglicised to Lord Louis Mountbatten.

BIBLIOGRAPHY

A History of the 2nd Battalion, The Monmouthshire Regiment compiled by Captain G. A. Brett, D.S.O., M.C. Hughes & Son, Pontypool. 1933.

A Territorial Soldier's War by Bryan Latham. Gale & Polden Ltd, Aldershot. 1967

A Year on the Western Front by J. Underhill. Facsimile edition, London Press Exchange Ltd. 1988.

Chronicle of Youth, Vera Brittain's War Diary 1913-1917. Victor Gollancz Ltd. 1981

Four Years on the Western Front by A Rifleman. Odhams Press Ltd., London. 1922.

Gentlemen and Officers by K. W. Mitchinson. Imperial War Museum Department of Printed Books. 1995

Goodbye to All That by Robert Graves J. Cape, London. 1929

Gunner on the Western Front by Aubrey Wade. Revised Edition. B. T. Batsford Ltd, London. 1959.

History of the East Lancashire Regiment in the Great War 1914-1918. Littelbury Bros. Ltd., Liverpool. 1936.

History of the London Rifle Brigade 1859-1919. Constable & Co. Ltd., London. 1921.

History of the Royal Irish Rifles by Cyral Falls. Gale & Polden, Aldershot. 1925

Official History of Australia in the War of 1914-1918, Vol. IV. The A.I.F. in France 1917 by C. E. W. Bean.Angus & Robertson Ltd., Sydney. 1933.

Official History of the War, Military Operations France and Belgium 1914, Vol. II. Compiled by Brig. Gen. J. E. Edmonds C.B., C.M.G., R.E. (Retired), p.s.c. MacMillan & Co. Ltd., London. 1925.

Official History of the War, Military Operations France and Belgium 1917, Vol. II. Compiled by Brig.-Gen. J. E. Edmonds C.B., C.M.G., R.E. (Retired), p.s.c. H.M.S.O., London. 1948.

Short History of the London Rifle Brigade. Compiled Regimentally Gale & Polden Ltd., Aldershot. 1916

Silent Cities. Compiled by Sidney C. Hurst, P.A.S.I. Methuan & Co. Ltd. London. 1929

Testament of Youth by Vera Brittain. Victor Gollanz Ltd., London. 8th Impression 1935

The 2nd Munsters in France by Lieut.-Col.H. S. Jervis, M.C. Gale & Polden Ltd, Aldershot. 1922.

A History of The 2nd Battalion, The Monmouthshire Regiment. Compiled by Captain G. A. Brett, D.S.O., M.C. The South Wales Borderers (24th Regiment). Hughes and Son, Pontypool. 1933.

BIBLIOGRAPHY

Regimental Records of the Royal Welch Fusiliers (23rd Regiment), Vol. III 1914-1918 France and Flanders compiled by C. H. Dudley Ward, D.S.O., M.C. Forster Groom & CO. Ltd., London. 1928.

The Battle Book of Ypres. Compiled by Beatrix Brice.
John Murray, London. 1927.

The Bond of Sacrifice Vol. I Aug–Dec., 1914.
Anglo-African Publishing Contractors. London. 1916.

The Book of The 7th [S] Battalion, Royal Inniskilling Fusiliers from Tipperary to Ypres by G. A. Cooper Walker. Brindley & Son Dublin. 1920.

The Die-Hards in the Great War. Vol I 1914-1916 by Everard Wirrall.
Harrison & Sons Ltd, London. 1926.

The Great War Diaries of Brigadier General Alexander Johnston 1914-1917 by Edwin Astill. Pen & Sword Books Ltd. 2007.

The Grenadier Guards in the Great War 1914-1918 Vol. I. by Lieut.-Col. The Right Hon. Sir Francis Ponsonby. Macmillan & Co. Ltd., London. 1920.

The History of the 2/6th Lancashire Fusiliers by Captain C. H. Potter, M.C. and Capt. A. S. C. Fothergill. The 'Observer' General Printing Works, Rochdale.1927.

The History of the 36th (Ulster) Division by Cyril Falls.
M'Caw, Stevenson & Orr, Ltd., Belfast. 1922.

The History of the 47th (london) Division 1914-1919 edited by Alan H Maude. Amalgamated Press Ltd., London. 1922.

The History of the Cheshire Regiment in the Great war 1914-1918 by Arthur Crookenden, Colonel of the Regiment.W. H. Evans, Sons & Co. Ltd., Cheshire.

The History of the London Rifle Brigade 1859–1919 with introduction by Maj.-Gen. Sir Frederick Maurice K.C.M.G., C.B.
Constable & Company Ltd., London. 1921.

The History of the Rifle Brigade in the War of 1914-1919 Vol. I, August 1914-December 1916 by Reginald Berkeley, M.C.The Rifle Brigade Club Ltd., London. 1927.

The History of the Second Division 1914-1918 Vol I 1914-1916 by Everard Wyrall. Thomas Nelson & Sons Ltd. London. 1921

The History of the Somerset Light Infantry (Prince Albert's) 1914-1919 by Edward Wyrall. Methuen & Co. Ltd. London. 1927.

The Immortal Heritage by Fabian Ware.
Cambridge University Press. 1937

The Irish Guards in the Great War Vol. I by Rudyard Kipling.
Macmillan & Co. Limited., London. 1923.

The Irish Regiments in the First World War by Henry Harris.
The Mercher Press, Cork. 1968.

BIBLIOGRAPHY

The King's Pilgrimage. Hodder and Stoughton Ltd., London. 1922.

The L.R.B. Record, The Journal of the London Rifle Brigade. No. 134 April, No. 136 June, No. 137 July, No. 138 August 1927 and No. 206 April 1933

The Long Carry. The War Diary of Stretcher Bearer Frank Dunham 1916-1918. Edited by R. H. Haigh and P. W Turner. Pergamon Press.1970.

The Micks. The Story of the Irish Guards by Peter Verney. Peter Davis, London. 1970.

The Rifle Brigade Chronicle for 1914. Compiled and Edited by Col. Willough by Verner. John Bale, Sons & Danielson Ltd., London. 1915.

The Rifle Brigade Chronicle for 1915. Compiled and Edited by Col. Willough by Verner. John Bale, Sons & Danielson Ltd., London. 1916.

The Royal Inniskilling Fusiliers in the World War by Sir Frank Fox, O.B.E. Constable & Co. Ltd., London. 1928.

The Story of the Household Cavalry. Captain Sir George Arthur Bart. William Heinemman Ltd., London, 1926.

The Silent Cities. Compiled with the kind permission of The Imperial War Graves Commission by Sidney Hurst. Methuen & Co. Ltd. London 1929.

The Times History of the War Vol XV. Printed and Published by 'The Times', London. 1918.

The Unending Vigil by Philip Longworth. Constable & C0. Ltd., London. 1967.

The War the Infantry Knew 1914-1919 by one of their Medical Officers (Captain J. C. Dunn). P. S. King & Son Ltd. London. 1938

The Worcestershire Regiment in the Great War by Captain H. FitzM. Stacke, MC forming part of The Worcestershire War Memorial. G. T. Cheshire & Sons Ltd., Kidderminster. 1928

Private Papers.
Patrik Indevuyst
Andy Mackay
Dennis Otter
Ted Smith
Tony Spagnoly
Peter Threlfall
Philip Woets

INDEX

INDEX

INDEX

INDEX

INDEX

INDEX